MONDAY Patterning and Algebra

1 Use the array to find the product.

6 × 2 = _____

○○○○○○
○○○○○○

3 What is the missing number?

7 + _____ = 14

4 What is the next number if the pattern rule is add 7?

14, _____

2 Draw 3 groups of 4 crayons.

How many crayons are there? _____

Write the sentence for 3 groups of 4.

_____ × _____ = 12

5 Extend the pattern.

10, 20, 30, _____, _____, _____

What is the pattern rule?

_____

TUESDAY Number Sense and Operations

1   4 7 2
      + 3 5 8

3 Round the following numbers to the nearest 10.

A. 67 _____

B. 25 _____

5 What is the value of the coins?

_____

2 Circle the greatest number.

47   32   11

4 What is the number?

_____

WEDNESDAY Geometry

1 What is the name of this shape?

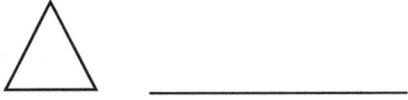

_____

2 How many right angles does a square have?

_____

3 What is the name of this 3D shape?

_____

4 Draw a line of symmetry.

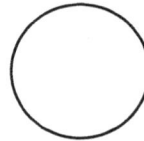

5 Circle the hexagon.

THURSDAY Measurement

1 The time is 4:15. What time will it be in 30 minutes? Use a clock model to help you.

_____ : _____

3 Which shape has the greatest area?

A. _____   B. _____   C. _____

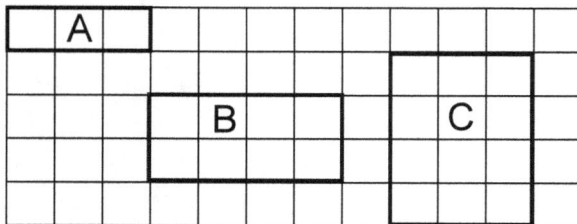

2 Find the perimeter and the area of the shaded shape.

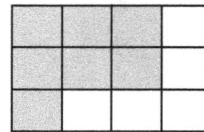

The perimeter is _____ units.

The area is _____ square units.

4 How many days in a week?

A. 5 days   B. 6 days   C. 7 days

Here are the results of a survey on favourite colours.
Complete the chart and answer the questions about the results.

Colour	Tally	Number
Red	卌 ||	
Blue	卌 卌 |||	
Green	||||	
Purple	卌 ||	

1 What was the most popular colour? _____

2 What was the least popular colour? _____

3 How many people liked either green or purple? _____

4 How many people were surveyed? _____

5 Which colours did the same number of people like most? _____

BRAIN STRETCH

Jane has 24 red beads and 52 blue beads.
How many beads does she have altogether?

MONDAY — Patterning and Algebra

1 What is the missing number?

____ + 5 = 11

2 Which number sentence has the same difference as 10 – 7?

A. 4 – 2   B. 8 – 6   C. 6 – 3

3 What is the next number if the pattern rule is subtract 4?

12, ____

4 Eliza bought 8 packages of granola bars. Each package has 5 granola bars. Draw an array to find the product.

8 × 5 = ____

5 Extend the pattern.

110, 120, 130, _____, _____, _____

TUESDAY — Number Sense and Operations

1
```
  89
– 45
```

2 Circle the greatest number.

905   239   932

3 Round the following numbers to the nearest 10.

A. 82 _____

B. 39 _____

4 The numeral for thirty is:

A. 80   B. 70   C. 30

5 Write an addition sentence that equals 4 × 4. Include the sum.

WEDNESDAY Geometry

1 Which of these shapes is not a quadrilateral?

A. triangle   B. rhombus

C. rectangle   D. square

2 How many sides does an octagon have?

_____

3 What is the name of this 3D shape?

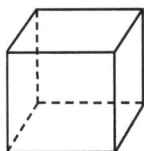

_____

4 Draw 2 lines of symmetry.

X

5 Draw a rectangle.

THURSDAY Measurement

1 What time is it?

_____

2 How many hours in a day?

A. 30 hours   B. 24 hours   C. 12 hours

3 Find the perimeter and the area of the shaded shape.

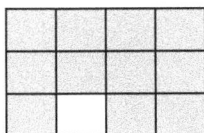

The perimeter is _____ units.

The area is _____ square units.

4 What is the best unit of measure for the length of a shoe?

A. kilometres   B. metres   C. centimetres

Iris surveyed her classmates about their favourite meal.

1 Use the information from Iris's survey to complete the tally chart.

Favourite Meal Survey

Name	Meal
Roy	lunch
Jody	dinner
Patrick	dinner
Timothy	dinner
Rachel	lunch
Sam	dinner
Kara	lunch
Kendra	breakfast
Jeremy	breakfast
Lisa	lunch
Juan	dinner

Favourite Meal

Meal	Tally
breakfast	
lunch	
dinner	

2 Which meal did the most students choose? _____

3 Which meal did the fewest students choose? _____

4 How many students did Iris survey? _____

BRAIN STRETCH

1
```
   78
+ 11
```

2
```
   89
-  45
```

3
```
   37
+ 62
```

4
```
   54
-  34
```

MONDAY Patterning and Algebra

1 What is the next number if the pattern rule is subtract 6?

30, _____

2 Which number sentence has the same difference as 5 – 2?

A. 4 – 2   B. 8 – 6   C. 6 – 3

3 Barry wants to set 6 chairs around each of 4 tables. How many chairs will he need? Draw an array to find the product.

6 × 4 = _____

4 Extend the pattern.

11, 22, 33, _____, _____

TUESDAY Number Sense and Operations

1
```
    168
  + 234
```

2 Write the following numbers in expanded form.

A. 398 _____

B. 651 _____

3 What is the value of the underlined digit?

A. <u>9</u>01 _____

B. 56<u>2</u> _____

4 Compare the numbers using <, >, or =.

345 [ ] 585

WEDNESDAY Geometry

1 Describe the angle.

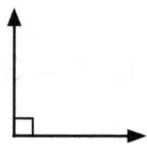

A. right angle

B. greater than a right angle

C. less than a right angle

3 How many lines of symmetry?

C

_____

2 What is the name of this 3D shape?

_____

4 How many sides does a triangle have?

_____

5 What 3D shape could be made from these pieces?

A. cylinder   B. rectangular prism   C. pyramid

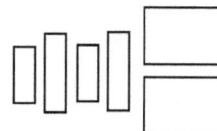

THURSDAY Measurement

1 What is the symbol for the word metre?

A, cm   B. m   C. km

2 How many minutes in 1 hour?

A. 30 mins   B. 60 mins   C. 100 mins

3 Find the perimeter and the area of the shaded shape.

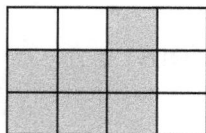

The perimeter is _____ units.

The area is _____ square units.

4 What is the best unit of measure for the length of an ant?

A. metres

B. centimetres

C. millimetres

FRIDAY Data Management

Here are the results of a survey on favourite drinks.
Use the pictograph to answer the questions about the results.

Favourite Drinks

Lemonade	
Milk	
Orange Juice	

Key: = 2 people

1 How many people were surveyed? _____

2 Which drink did the fewest people choose? _____

3 Which two drinks were chosen by the same number of people?

_____

4 How many more people chose milk than chose orange juice? _____

BRAIN STRETCH

1	**2**	**3**	**4**
56 + 26	85 − 19	27 + 64	54 − 19

MONDAY — Patterning and Algebra

1 What is the missing number?

_____ + 9 = 10

2 Which number sentence has the same sum as 10 + 6?

A. 4 + 9   B. 8 + 8   C. 9 + 9

3 There are 8 groups of 3 rulers for the class. How many rulers are there? Draw an array to find the product.

8 × 3 = _____

4 Alex has 6 boxes of balls. There are 5 balls in each box.

How many balls are there? _____

Use a model to help solve.

TUESDAY — Number Sense and Operations

1 Are these numbers even or odd?

A. 65 _____

B. 108 _____

2 Write the following numbers in expanded form.

A. 241

_____

B. 386

_____

3 What is the value of the coins?

_____

4 What fraction names the shaded part?

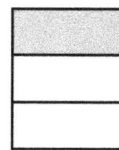

A. $\frac{1}{2}$ B. $\frac{1}{3}$ C. $\frac{1}{4}$

Week 4

WEDNESDAY Geometry

1 What is the name of this shape?

◯ _____

2 How many vertices does a pentagon have?

_____

3 What is the name of this 3D shape?

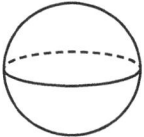

_____

4 Describe the angle.

A. right angle

B. greater than a right angle

C. less than a right angle

5 Look at these shapes. Choose flip or slide.

☺ → ☺   A. flip   B. slide

THURSDAY Measurement

1 What is the symbol for the word kilometre?

A. cm   B. m   C. km

2 Draw a line 1 cm long.

3 Find the perimeter and the area of the shaded shape.

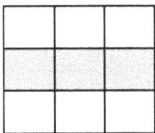

The perimeter is _____ units.

The area is _____ square units.

4 How many minutes in 2 hours?

A. 30 mins

B. 60 mins

C. 120 mins

Here are the results of a survey on favourite ice cream flavours.
Use the pictograph to answer the questions about the results

Favourite Ice Cream Flavours

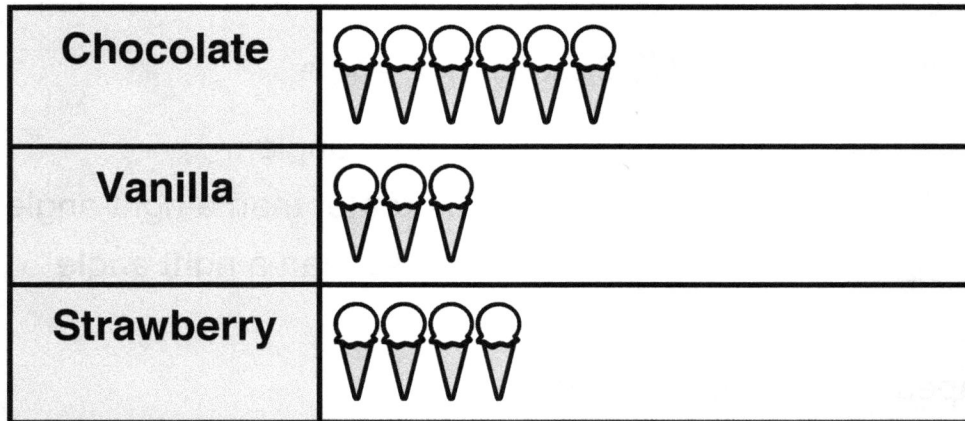

Chocolate	🍦🍦🍦🍦🍦🍦
Vanilla	🍦🍦🍦
Strawberry	🍦🍦🍦🍦

Key: 🍦 = 5 people

1 What flavour of ice cream was the most popular? _____

2 What flavour of ice cream was the least popular? _____

3 How many people chose either vanilla or strawberry? _____

4 How many people were surveyed? _____

BRAIN STRETCH

Thomas has a collection of 100 stamps.
He buys 3 more packages of stamps.
Each package has 10 stamps.
How many stamps does Thomas now have in his collection?

MONDAY — Patterning and Algebra

1 Write related addition and multiplication sentences.

4 groups of 8

_____ + _____ + _____ + _____ = _____

_____ × _____ = _____

3 What is the missing number?

_____ − 7 = 8

5 What is the next number if the pattern rule is add 7?

22, _____

2 Which number sentence has the same difference as 15 − 6?

A. 12 − 2

B. 10 − 1

C. 6 − 3

4 You have 20 stickers. Put 5 stickers in each box. How many boxes did you fill?

TUESDAY — Number Sense and Operations

1 Write the following numbers in expanded form.

A. 974 _____

B. 413 _____

2
$$816 - 434$$

3 How many equal parts in the whole?

_____ equal parts

4 Compare the numbers using <, >, or =.

230 ☐ 420

WEDNESDAY Geometry

1 What is the name of this shape?

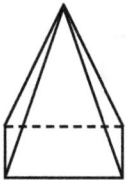
_____

2 How many vertices does a rhombus have?

_____

3 What is the name of this 3D shape?

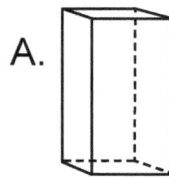
_____

4 Which 3D shape can roll?

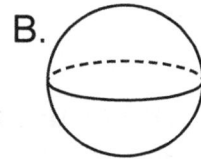

A.   B.   C.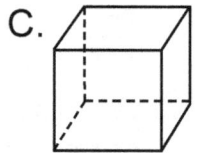

THURSDAY Measurement

1 What is the symbol for millimetre?

_____

2 Draw a line 2 cm long.

3 Find the perimeter and the area of the shaded shape.

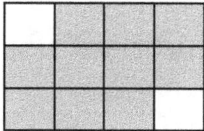

The perimeter is _____ units.

The area is _____ square units.

4

It is ____ : ____.

In 15 minutes, it will be ____ : ____.

Data Management

Here are the results of a survey on favourite pets.
Complete the chart and answer the questions about the results.

Pet	Tally	Number
Dog	‖‖ ‖‖ ‖	
Cat	‖‖ ‖‖	
Hamster	‖‖ ‖‖	
Bird	‖‖	

1 What was the most popular pet? _____

2 What was the least popular pet? _____

3 How many students chose either a dog or bird? _____

4 How many more students chose a cat than a hamster? _____

5 How many fewer students chose a cat than a dog? _____

BRAIN STRETCH

Katherine picked 65 apples and 76 pears.
How many pieces of fruit did she pick in all?

MONDAY — Patterning and Algebra

1 Divide 10 into groups of 5.

$10 \div 5 =$ _____

2 Which number sentence has the same sum as 8 + 5?

A. 6 + 7   B. 4 + 3   C. 11 + 4

3 What is the missing number?

_____ − 10 = 4

4 Chloe was trying to find 54 ÷ 9. She said, "I know that 9 × 6 = 54, so 54 ÷ 9 must be 6."

Is Chloe correct? _____

Use pictures and words to help show why.

5 Multiply by 2.
2 × 1 = ___   2 × 2 = ___   2 × 3 = ___
2 × 4 = ___   2 × 5 = ___   2 × 6 = ___

Are the products even or odd?

_____

TUESDAY — Number Sense and Operations

1 Circle the odd number.

67   90

2 Write an addition sentence that equals 2 × 7. Include the sum.

3 Count back by 10s.

200, _____, _____, _____, _____

4 What fraction names the shaded part?

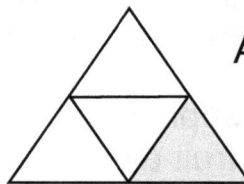

A. $\frac{1}{2}$ B. $\frac{1}{3}$ C. $\frac{1}{4}$

5 Write the following numbers in expanded form.

A. 651 _____

B. 742 _____

© Chalkboard Publishing

WEDNESDAY Geometry

1 What is the name of this shape?

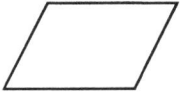

_____

2 How many sides does a trapezoid have?

_____

3 What is the name of this 3D shape?

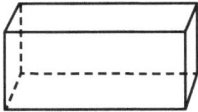

_____

4 Draw 2 lines of symmetry.

O

5 Which 3D shape has a square for a face?

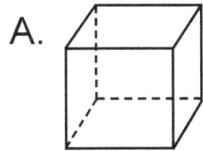

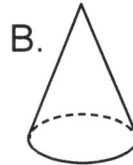

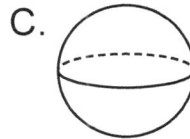

A.   B.   C.

THURSDAY Measurement

1 Circle the better estimate for the distance between schools.

A. cm   B. m   C. km

2 How many minutes are between 8:30 and 8:45?

8:30   8:35   8:40   8:45

3 Find the perimeter and the area of the shaded shape.

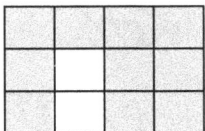

The perimeter is _____ units.

The area is _____ square units.

4 How many months in a year?

A. 100 months

B. 12 months

C. 20 months

FRIDAY Data Management

Andrew surveyed his classmates about their favourite snacks.

1 Use the information from Andrew's survey to complete the tally chart.

Favourite Snack Survey

Name	Snack
Maria	vegetables
Kevin	fruit
Becca	popcorn
Leo	vegetables
Mina	fruit
Patricia	crackers
Noah	popcorn
Ryan	fruit
Savanah	vegetables
Wayne	popcorn
Martin	fruit
Jessica	fruit

Favourite Snack

Snack	Tally
Vegetables	
Popcorn	
Fruit	
Crackers	

2 Which snack did the most students choose? _____

3 Which snack did the fewest students choose? _____

4 How many students did Andrew survey? _____

5 Which snack was chosen by only 1 student? _____

BRAIN STRETCH

The answer is 24. Show at least three ways to make 24 using any combination of −, +, ×, ÷, and = .

MONDAY Patterning and Algebra

1 Find the missing number.

9, 18, 27, _____, 45, 54, 63

2 Which number sentence has the same difference as 20 – 10?

A. 15 – 5   B. 18 – 9   C. 17 – 8

3 What is the missing number?

_____ – 3 = 11

4 Celia earns $8 a week. After 4 weeks, how much money does she have? _____

Give another situation that matches 8 × 4.

_____

_____

5 What is the next number if the pattern rule is subtract 5?

77, _____

TUESDAY Number Sense and Operations

1 What is the value of the underlined digit?

A. 6̲50 _____   B. 24̲2 _____

2   718
      – 279

3 Count back by 10s.

675, _____, _____, _____, _____

4 Compare the numbers using <, >, or =.

120 ☐ 229

5 Write an addition sentence that equals 1 × 5. Include the sum.

WEDNESDAY — Geometry

1 How many vertices?

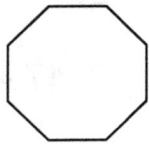

_____

2 How many sides does a quadrilateral have?

_____

3 Can this 3D shape be stacked?

A. yes

B. no

4 Describe the angle.

A. right angle

B. greater than a right angle

C. less than a right angle

5 What 3D shape does a ball look like?

_____

THURSDAY — Measurement

1 Which tool would you use to measure the temperature on a cold day?

A. scale   B. thermometre   C. ruler

2 How many minutes are between 3:20 and 3:30? Use a model to help you.

_____

3 Use two methods to find the area of the rectangle.

A. Count the unit squares. ___ square units

B. Multiply side lengths. 4 × ___ = ___ square units

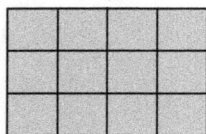

4 Order the temperatures from lowest to highest.

12°C, –4°C, 30°C

_____, _____, _____

Here are the results of a survey on favourite cookies.
Use the pictograph to answer the questions about the results.

Favourite Cookie Flavours

Chocolate Chip	🍪🍪🍪🍪
Oatmeal Raisin	🍪🍪
Gingerbread	🍪

Key: 🍪 = 5 people

1 How many people were surveyed? _____

2 Ten people liked _____.

3 How many fewer people like gingerbread than like chocolate chip? _____

4 How many more people like chocolate chip than like oatmeal raisin? _____

BRAIN STRETCH

Ivan is drawing a pattern using geometric shapes.
Here is his pattern:

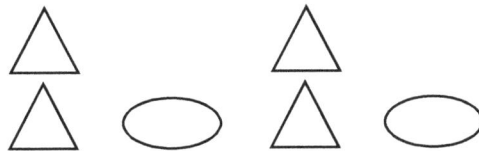

△   △
△ ◯ △ ◯

When Ivan has drawn 5 ovals, how many triangles will be in his pattern?

MONDAY Patterning and Algebra

1 Complete the fact family.

$4 \times 6 =$ ___ $24 \div 4 =$ ___

$6 \times$ ___ $= 24$ $24 \div 6 =$ ___

3 Draw an array. Write a division sentence and solve it.

20 circles in 4 rows

____ ÷ ____ = ____

2 Which number sentence has the same sum as $7 + 7$?

A. $6 + 9$ B. $7 + 3$ C. $9 + 5$

4 Extend the pattern.

5, 10, 15, 20, _____, _____, _____

What do you notice about multiples of 5?

_____

TUESDAY Number Sense and Operations

1 What is the value of the underlined digit?

A. 8̲52 _____

B. 30̲7 _____

2 Which number would be rounded to 60?

A. 64   B. 65   C. 53

3 What fraction names the shaded part?

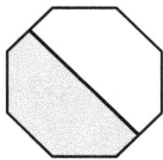

A. $\frac{1}{2}$ B. $\frac{1}{3}$ C. $\frac{1}{4}$

4 Draw lines on the shape to show fourths.

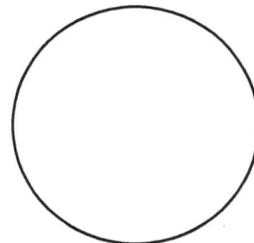

WEDNESDAY Geometry

1 Draw a circle.

2 A rhombus is a quadrilateral.

   A. true   B. false

3 What 3D shape does this juice can look like?

_____

4 Which of the following is a point?

   A. ⟵————⟶

   B. •————•

   C. •

5 Which shape does not have a line of symmetry?

   A.   B.   C.

THURSDAY Measurement

1 How many metres in a kilometre?

_____

2 How many seconds in a minute?

   A. 30   B. 60   C. 120

3 Draw a line $1\frac{1}{2}$ cm long.

4 Find the perimeter and the area of the shaded shape.

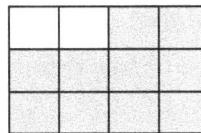

The perimeter is _____ units.

The area is _____ square units.

5 What is the best estimate for the length of a notebook?

   A. about 1 cm

   B. about 200 cm

   C. about 25 cm

Jose surveyed his classmates about their favourite field trips.

1 Use the information from Jose's survey to complete the tally chart.

Favourite Field Trip Survey

Name	Field Trip
Nicole	farm
Kevin	farm
Helen	science centre
Joseph	museum
Sara	factory
Charles	factory
Donna	farm
William	museum
Paul	farm
Wayne	museum
Angela	science centre
Brian	science centre

Favourite Field Trip

Field Trip	Tally
Science Centre	
Factory	
Museum	
Farm	

2 Did more students choose the farm or the museum? _____

3 Which field trip did the most students choose? _____

4 Which field trips did 3 students choose? _____

5 How many students did Jose survey? _____

BRAIN STRETCH

Kate had 340 marbles. She gave her friend Mark 78 marbles. How many marbles did she have left?

MONDAY Patterning and Algebra

1 What is the missing number?

_____ – 6 = 8

2 Which number sentence has the same difference as 30 – 22?

A. 12 – 4   B. 18 – 9   C. 12 – 3

3 Draw an array. Write a division sentence and solve it.

18 circles in 3 rows

_____ ÷ _____ = _____

4 Extend the pattern.

6, 12, 18, 24, _____, _____, _____

Six is an even number. What do you notice about multiples of even numbers?

_____

TUESDAY Number Sense and Operations

1 Write an addition sentence that equals 6 × 5. Include the sum.

2 Compare the numbers using <, >, or =.

785 ☐ 123

3 Count back by 10s.

393, _____, _____, _____, _____

4 Divide the rectangle to show fourths.

There are ___ equal parts. Each part is called one fourth or ___.

5 Write the following numbers in expanded form.

A. 766 _____

B. 647 _____

WEDNESDAY Geometry

1 What 3D shape does this ball look like?

_____

2 What is a polygon?

_____

_____

3 Draw a picture of a quadrilateral.

4 Draw a line of symmetry.

5 Look at these shapes. Choose flip, slide, or turn.

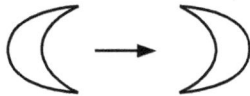

A. flip   B. slide   C. turn

THURSDAY Measurement

1 What is the better estimate for the weight of a watermelon?

A. 2 grams   B. 2 kilograms

2 Which distance is shorter than 1 km?

A. the distance between two desks

B. the distance between two cities

3 Find the perimeter and the area of the shaded shape.

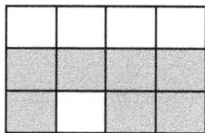

The perimeter is _____ units.

The area is _____ square units.

4 About how long is this line?

_____

A. about 1 cm

B. about 10 cm

C. about 1 m

© Chalkboard Publishing

FRIDAY Data Management

The Demaat family went apple picking. The bar graph shows how many apples each family member picked. Answer the questions.

Number of Apples Picked

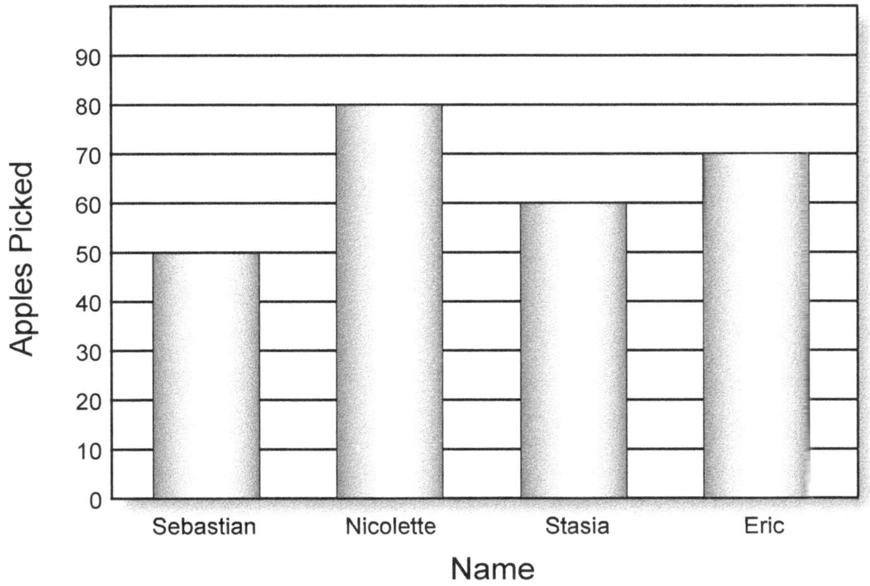

1 Who picked the most apples? ____________________

2 How many more apples did Nicolette pick than Sebastian? __________

3 Who picked 60 apples? ______________

4 How many members are there in the Demaat family? ____________

BRAIN STRETCH

If a horse has 4 legs, how many legs do 6 horses have?

MONDAY — Patterning and Algebra

1 Sam has 30 grapes. If he puts 6 grapes in each cup, how many cups can he fill? Use a model.
_____ cups

2 What is the missing number?

_____ + 10 = 20

3 What is the next number if the pattern rule is subtract 3?
86, _____

4 Write related addition and multiplication sentences.

5 groups of 6

_____ + _____ + _____ + _____ + _____ =

_____ × _____ = _____

TUESDAY — Number Sense and Operations

1 What number is 10 more than 457?

_____

2 Write the following numbers in expanded form.

A. 651 _____

B. 765 _____

3 Count on by 5s.

130, _____, _____, _____, _____

5 Write the number word for 523.

_____

4 A cake is cut into 4 equal parts. What is each equal part called?

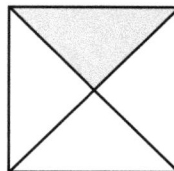

A. $\frac{1}{2}$ B. $\frac{1}{3}$ C. $\frac{1}{4}$

6 100 + 20 + 30 = _____

WEDNESDAY Geometry

1 What is a quadrilateral?

_____

_____

2 Draw a quadrilateral and a rhombus.

A. Give one way they are the same.

_____

B. Give one way they are different.

_____

3 What 3D shape does this die look like?

_____

4 Draw a line of symmetry.

W

5 What 3D shape could be made from these pieces?

A. cylinder   B. rectangular prism   C. pyramid

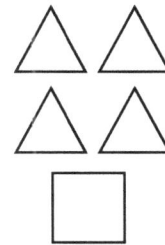

THURSDAY Measurement

1 Circle the better estimate of how much an orange weighs.

A. 2 kilograms   B. 200 grams

2 How many minutes are between 9:20 and 10:00? Count by 10s and complete the number line.

9:20 ____ ____ ____ 10:00

3 Find the perimeter and the area of the shaded shape.

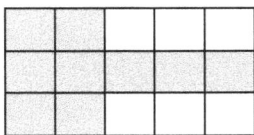

The perimeter is _____ units.

The area is _____ square units.

4 How many days in 10 weeks?

A. 100 days

B. 50 days

C. 70 days

Antonio and Sharon planted a flower garden. The bar graph shows how many of each flower they planted. Answer the questions.

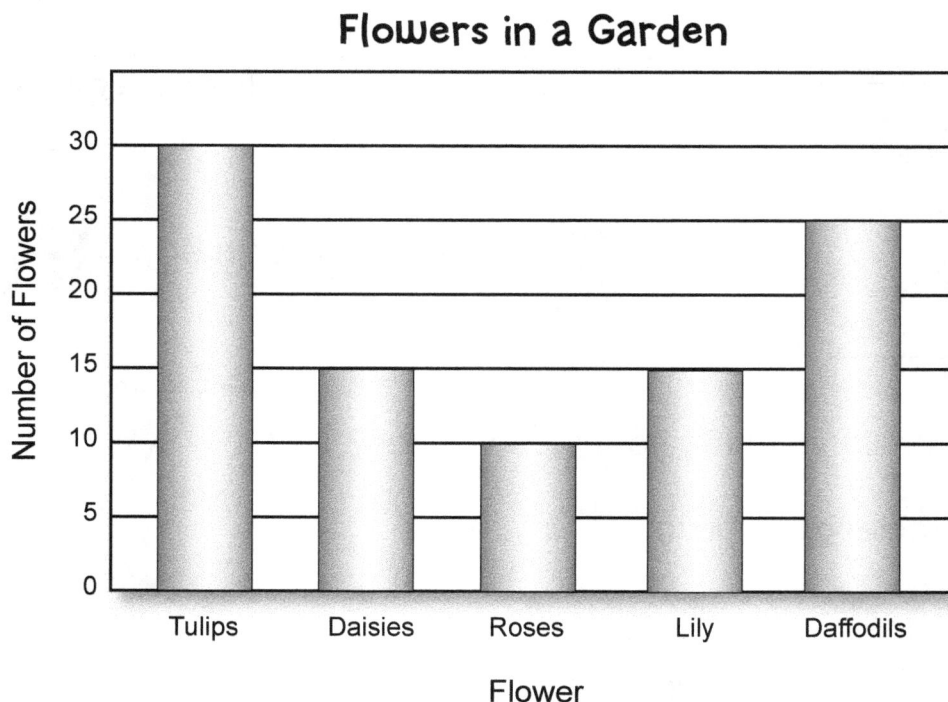

Flowers in a Garden

1 How many fewer daffodils were planted than tulips? _____

2 How many roses were planted? _____

3 How many more daisies were planted than roses? _____

4 Which flower was planted the most? _____

5 How many lilies were planted? _____

BRAIN STRETCH

How many eggs are there in 3 dozen?

MONDAY — Patterning and Algebra

1 Write two multiplication sentences for the array.

OOOOO
OOOOO

_____ × _____ = _____

_____ × _____ = _____

3 Which number sentence has the same difference as 17 − 5?

A. 14 − 3   B. 18 − 4   C. 20 − 8

2 Draw an array. Write a division sentence and solve it.

14 circles in 2 rows

_____ ÷ _____ = _____

4 There are 15 apples. If you share the apples equally with 3 friends, how many apples will each one get?

_____

Draw a situation that shows 3 groups of 5.

TUESDAY — Number Sense and Operations

1 What number is 10 less than 417?

_____

3 Count on by 2s.

422, _____, _____, _____, _____

5 Order the numbers from least to greatest.

670, 607, 706

_____ < _____ < _____

2 Are these numbers odd or even?

A.   12 _____

B.   29 _____

4 Circle $\frac{1}{3}$ of the group.

6 Colour parts of the shape to show $\frac{7}{8}$.

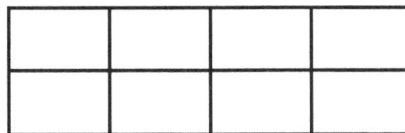

WEDNESDAY Geometry

1 Name a shape that has 5 sides.

_____

3 What 3D shape does this hat look like?

_____

5 Circle the polygons.

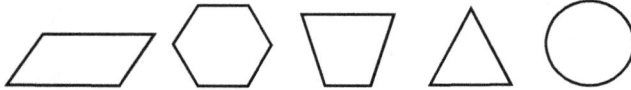

2 Are these shapes congruent?

A. yes
B. no

4 Draw a quadrilateral and a parallelogram.

A. Give one way they are the same.

_____

B. Give one way they are different.

_____

THURSDAY Measurement

1 What is the better estimate of the temperature on a cold snowy day?

A. 0°C   B. 30°C

3 Find the perimeter and the area of the shaded shape.

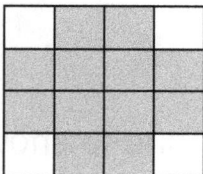

The perimeter is _____ units.

The area is _____ square units.

2 Draw a line 2 cm long.

4 The time is 12:30 p.m. What time will it be in 45 minutes?

A. 1:00 p.m.

B. 1:15 p.m.

C. 1:30 p.m.

FRIDAY Data Management

This chart shows the number of students and desks in each third grade class.

Teacher	Ms. Apor	Mr. Patel	Mrs. Smith	Ms. Rocco
Number of Students	25	22	24	25
Number of Desks	25	20	24	27

1 Whose class needs more desks? _____

2 Which two teachers have the same number of students?

_____

3 Which teacher has more desks than students? _____

4 Who has the fewest number of students? _____

5 Who has the most number of students? _____

BRAIN STRETCH

Helen has 30 tulips to plant in her garden.
Show 2 different ways she can arrange the tulips into rows of equal length.
Write a division sentence for each way she can arrange the tulips.

MONDAY — Patterning and Algebra

1 What is the missing number?

7 + ____ = 18

2 Which number sentence has the same answer as 22 − 10?

A. 6 + 2   B. 8 + 4   C. 10 + 1

3 Draw an array. Write a division sentence and solve it.

25 circles in 5 rows

4 Chad said, "All the multiples of 10 end in 0." Is he correct? Use examples to help show why.

_____

_____

____ ÷ ____ = ____

5 What is the next number if the pattern rule is add 7?   14, ____

TUESDAY — Number Sense and Operations

1 Estimate and then solve the sum.

```
        589
Estimate _____  + 270
```

2 Are these numbers odd or even?

A. 374 _____

B.   67 _____

3 Subtract.

20 − 5 − 10 =

4 What is the number?

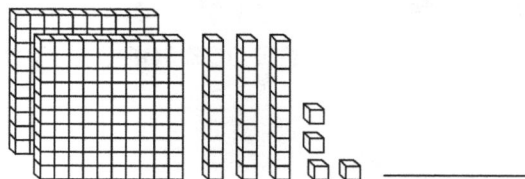

5 Order the numbers from greatest to least.

899, 901, 818

_____ > _____ > _____

6 Colour parts of the shape to show $\frac{1}{6}$.

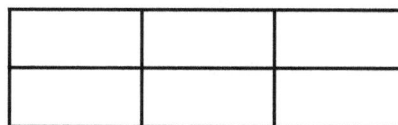

WEDNESDAY Geometry

1 Name a shape that has 4 sides.

_____

2 How many vertices does a hexagon have?

_____

3 How many faces?

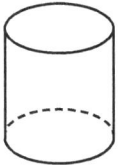

_____

4 Does this picture show a line of symmetry?

A. yes

B. no

5 Circle the quadrilaterals.

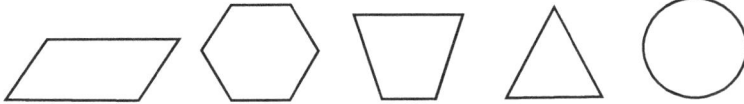

THURSDAY Measurement

1 What measuring tool would use to weigh something?

_____

3 Find the perimeter and the area of the shaded shape.

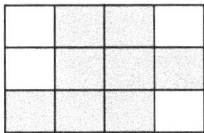

The perimeter is _____ units.

The area is _____ square units.

2 The time is 9:00 a.m.
What time will it be in 4 hours?

A. 1:00 p.m.

B. 1:15 p.m.

C. 1:30 p.m.

4 What is the best unit of measure for the height of a school?

A. milimetres

B. centimetres

C. metres

FRIDAY   Data Management

Here are the results of a survey on favourite breakfast foods.

1 Complete the chart and bar graph and answer the questions.

Favourite Breakfast Foods

Favourite Breakfast Foods	Tally	Number
Cereal		5
Eggs		15
Pancakes		20
Grilled Cheese		15

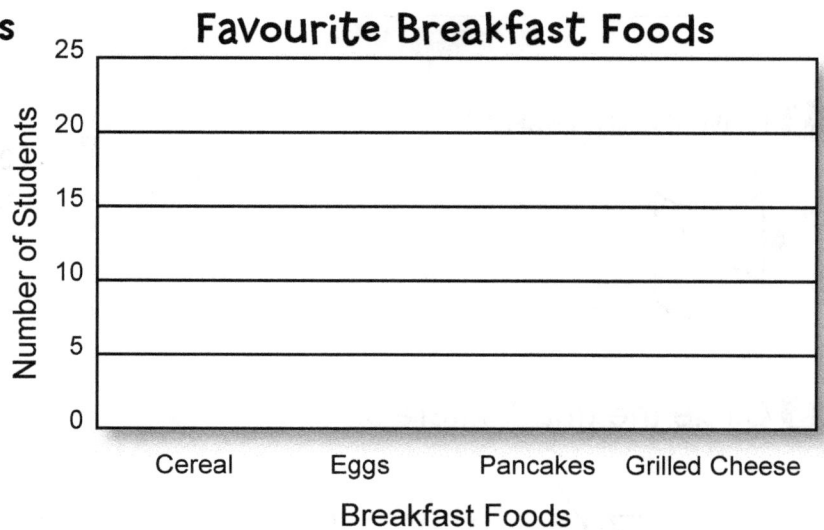

Favourite Breakfast Foods

Number of Students (0, 5, 10, 15, 20, 25)

Breakfast Foods: Cereal, Eggs, Pancakes, Grilled Cheese

2 What was the most popular breakfast food? _____

3 How many people liked either cereal or pancakes? _____

4 Which breakfast foods did the same number of people like?

_____

5 How many fewer people chose cereal than chose eggs? _____

BRAIN STRETCH

1	718	**2**	835	**3**	287	**4**	544
	+ 288		− 299		+ 634		− 198

MONDAY — Patterning and Algebra

1 What number comes next?

3, 6, 9, 12, 15, _____

What is the pattern rule?

_____

2 Which number sentence has the same answer as 14 − 7?

A. 6 + 2   B. 5 + 2   C. 10 − 5

3 What is the missing number?

_____ + 4 = 12

4 Is this a growing, shrinking, or repeating pattern?

_____

5 What is the next number if the pattern rule is subtract 4?

41, _____

TUESDAY — Number Sense and Operations

1 6 × 10 = _____

2 The rectangle has ___ equal parts.
Each part is called one third or ___.

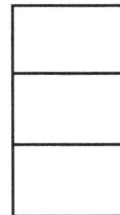

3 Write each amount in decimal form.

A. three dollars and sixty cents _____

B. twenty dollars and five cents _____

4 Compare the two fractions. Choose > or <.

$\frac{2}{8}$ ☐ $\frac{7}{8}$

5 Which creature is first in the row?

A. 🐢   B. 🐻   C. 🐨

WEDNESDAY Geometry

1 Draw a quadrilateral that is not a rectangle.

2 How many vertices does a triangle have?

_____

3 How many vertices?

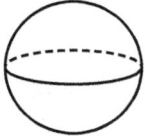

_____

4 Does this shape have a line of symmetry?

A. yes

B. no

5 Describe the following pair of lines.

A. parallel   B. intersecting   C. perpendicular

THURSDAY Measurement

1 What will the time be 30 minutes from now?

_____

2 Find the perimeter and the area of the shaded shape.

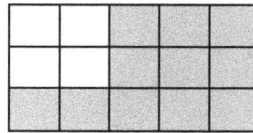

The perimeter is _____ units.

The area is _____ square units.

3 Which measuring tool would you use to find a date?

A. calendar

B. ruler

C. scale

4 Order the temperatures from lowest to highest.

33°C, 12°C, −3°C

_____, _____, _____

Ben went fishing. Look at the chart to see the number of fish Ben caught between Monday and Friday.

Day of the Week	Monday	Tuesday	Wednesday	Thursday	Friday
Number of Fish Caught	2	4	6	8	10

1 On what day did Ben catch the most number of fish? _____

2 On what day did Ben catch the least number of fish? _____

3 What kind of pattern do you notice? _____

4 How many fish did Ben catch on Tuesday and Thursday? _____

5 What is the difference between the most number of fish Ben caught and the fewest number of fish? _____

BRAIN STRETCH

Sophie had 192 tulip bulbs to plant.
She planted 49 tulip bulbs.
How many tulip bulbs still need to be planted?

MONDAY — Patterning and Algebra

1 Find the missing number.

111, 121, 131, _____, 151, 161

2 Which number sentence has the same answer as 3 × 3?

A. 8 + 2   B. 8 + 1   C. 10 − 6

3 Extend the pattern.

22, 27, 32, _____, _____, _____

4 Is this a growing, shrinking, or repeating pattern?

_____

5 What is the next number if the pattern rule is add 8?

54, _____

TUESDAY — Number Sense and Operations

1 Write the number word for 50.

_____

2 Count on by 10s.

901, _____, _____, _____, _____

3 Which is larger?
A. $\frac{1}{5}$ of a pizza

B. $\frac{1}{3}$ of a pizza.

How do you know? _____

_____

4 Circle $\frac{2}{4}$ of the group.

5 What number comes just before 268?

_____

WEDNESDAY Geometry

1 Draw a quadrilateral.

2 Name a shape that is not a quadrilateral.

_____

3 How many edges?

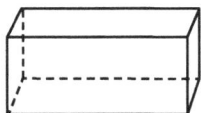

_____

4 Look at the shapes. Choose flip, slide, or turn.

A. flip   B. slide   C. turn

5 Describe the following pair of lines.

A. parallel   B. intersecting   C. perpendicular

THURSDAY Measurement

1 What time is it?

_____

2 Find the perimeter and the area of the shaded shape.

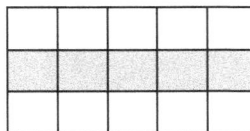

The perimeter is _____ units.

The area is _____ square units.

3 How much water could a bathtub hold? Circle the better estimate.

A. 80 millilitres   B. 80 litres

4 Which amount is lighter?

A. 10 grams   B. 10 kilograms

FRIDAY Data Management

Use data from the chart to complete the bar graph. Make sure you add labels!

Favourite Season Survey

Season	Number of Votes
Spring	10
Summer	15
Autumn	25
Winter	15

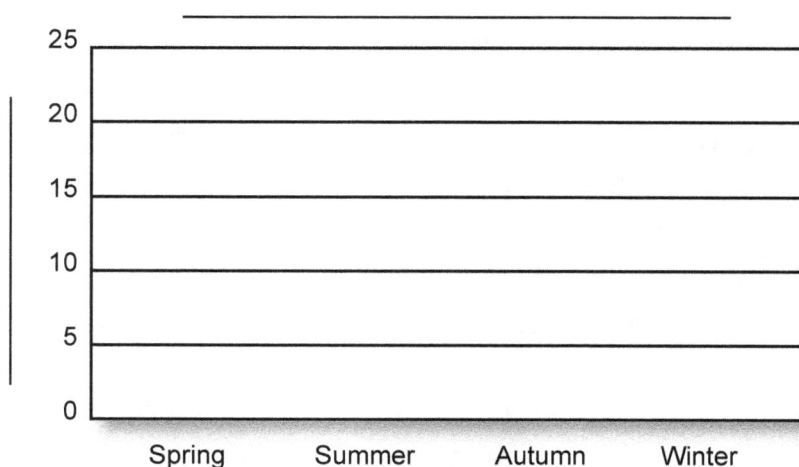

_____

25	
20	
15	
10	
5	
0	

Spring   Summer   Autumn   Winter

_____

1 List the seasons in order from the most votes to the fewest votes.

_____

2 How many more people chose winter than chose spring? _____

3 How many people chose either summer or autumn? _____

BRAIN STRETCH

John collected 234 stamps. Avita collected 356 stamps.
How many stamps did they collect altogether?

MONDAY Patterning and Algebra

1 Find the missing number.

87, 77, 67, _____, 47, 37

2 Which number sentence has the same quotient as $30 \div 6$?

A. $14 \div 2$ B. $25 \div 5$ C. $24 \div 6$

3 Ahdri has 9 packages of juice boxes. Each package has 3 juice boxes. Draw an array to find the product.

$9 \times 3 =$ _____

4 What number comes next?

335, 340, 345, _____

5 The table shows multiplying by 0. What is the pattern when you multiply a number by 0?

×	0	1	2	3	4	5
0	0	0	0	0	0	0

TUESDAY Number Sense and Operations

1 Write the numeral for:

500 + 20 + 2

_____

2 Write an addition sentence that equals 6×7. Include the sum.

3 Round the following numbers to the nearest 10.

A. 91 _____

B. 29 _____

4 Draw lines on the shape to show thirds.

5   7 8 9
    + 1 5 5
    ‾‾‾‾‾‾‾‾

WEDNESDAY Geometry

1 Draw a trapezoid.

2 How many lines of symmetry does this number have?

9 _____

3 How many faces?

_____

4 Does this shape have a line of symmetry?

A. yes
B. no

5 What 3D shape could be made from these pieces?

A. cone   B. cube   C. pyramid

THURSDAY Measurement

1 The time is 6:15. What time will it be in 20 minutes? Use a clock model to help you.

3 You can divide a shape into 2 parts to help find the area.

4 × __ = __ and 3 × __ = __

Add. The total area is 8 + __ = __ square units.

4

2

2

3

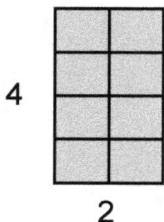

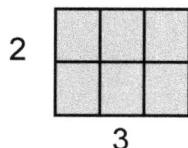

2 Find the perimeter and the area of the shaded shape.

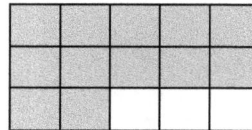

The perimeter is _____ units.

The area is _____ square units.

4 One litre of water fills 4 glasses. How many litres will it take to fill 8 glasses?

_____ litres

© Chalkboard Publishing

Here are the results of a survey on favourite farm animals.

Animal	Tally	Number
Chickens	‖‖‖ ‖‖‖ ‖	
Cows	‖‖‖	
Pigs	‖‖‖ ‖‖‖ ‖‖‖	
Horses	‖‖‖ ‖‖‖ ‖‖‖ ‖‖	
Sheep	‖‖‖	

1 How many people participated in the survey? _____

2 Which animal was the most popular? _____

3 How many more people chose horses than chose cows? _____

4 How many animals were chosen by the same number
of people? _____

5 How many people chose either chickens or pigs? _____

BRAIN STRETCH

Mathew had 5 book shelves. On each shelf he put 10 books.
How many books were on the book shelves altogether?

MONDAY — Patterning and Algebra

1 Multiply.

$1 \times 1 =$ ___ $1 \times 2 =$ ___ $1 \times 3 =$ ___

$1 \times 4 =$ ___ $1 \times 5 =$ ___ $1 \times 6 =$ ___

What is the pattern when you multiply a number by 1?

_____

3 What number comes next?

52, 50, 48, _____

2 Which number sentence has the same sum as 10 + 7?

A. 6 + 11   B. 8 + 8   C. 11 + 9

4 Draw an array.
Write a division sentence and solve it.

30 circles in 5 rows

_____ ÷ _____ = _____

TUESDAY — Number Sense and Operations

1 What is the value of the underlined digit?

A. 702 _____

B. 461 _____

2 Write each amount in decimal form.

four dollars and twenty-five cents

_____

two dollars and ten cents _____

3 What is the greater number?

A. eighty

B. 87

4 What is the number?

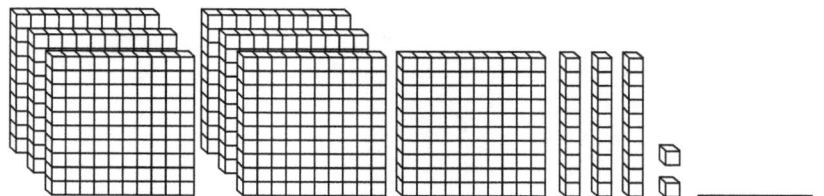

_____

WEDNESDAY Geometry

1 Name a 3D shape that can be stacked.

_____

2 How many vertices does an octagon have?

_____

3 How many vertices?

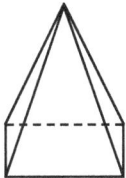

_____

4 Look at the shapes. Choose flip, slide, or turn.

A. flip   B. slide   C. turn

5 Circle the quadrilaterals.

THURSDAY Measurement

1 What is the best unit of measure for the length of a grasshopper?

_____

2 Ali wants to find the area of a tile. How many square cm is it?

5 cm 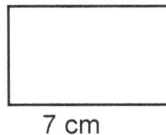   _____ square cm

7 cm

3 Find the perimeter and the area of the shaded shape.

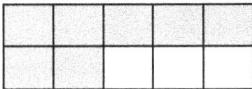

The perimeter is _____ units.

The area is _____ square units.

4 Kate uses litres and millilitres when she is baking.

A. Which one would she use to measure milk?

_____

B. Which one would she use to measure salt?

_____

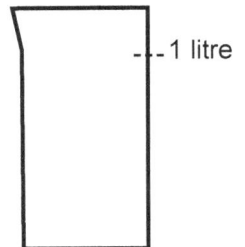
-- 1 litre

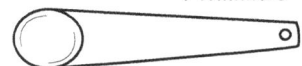
1 millilitre

FRIDAY   Data Management

The third grade class took a survey on favourite sports. They displayed the data as a pictograph. Use their pictograph to answer the questions.

Favourite Sports Survey

Soccer	☺ ☺ ☺ ☺
Basketball	☺ ☺ ☺ ☺ ☺ ☺ ☺ ☺
Hockey	☺ ☺ ☺ ☺ ☺

Key: ☺ = 3 votes

1 How many students liked soccer? _____

2 How many students liked basketball? _____

3 How many students liked hockey? _____

4 How many more students liked basketball than liked hockey? _____

5 List the sports from most favourite to least favourite.

_____

BRAIN STRETCH

Rafael has saved 24 dimes and 6 quarters.
Rafael is hoping to buy hockey cards that cost $5.60.
How many more dimes and quarters does Rafael need to buy his cards?

© Chalkboard Publishing

MONDAY — Patterning and Algebra

1 4 × 5 = 5 × 4

A. True   B. False

2 Which number sentence has the same product as 10 × 3?

A. 6 × 7   B. 6 × 5   C. 4 × 9

3 Is this a growing, shrinking, or repeating pattern?

_____

4 Draw an array. Write a division sentence and solve it.

28 circles in 4 rows

_____ ÷ _____ = _____

5 What is the next number if the pattern rule is subtract 3?   31, _____

TUESDAY — Number Sense and Operations

1 Write the numeral for:

900 + 40 + 3

_____

2 Round the following numbers to the nearest 10.

A. 48 _____

B. 75 _____

C. 22 _____

3 Vivian cuts a cake into 8 equal parts. What is each equal part called?

_____

4 Draw 15¢ using 3 coins.

5 Circle half of the group

WEDNESDAY Geometry

1 What does congruent mean?

_____

_____

2 Draw a rectangle and a square.

A. Give one way they are the same.

_____

B. Give one way they are different.

_____

3 How many vertices?

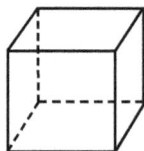

_____

4 Does this shape have a line of symmetry?

A. yes

B. no

5 What 3D shape could be made from these pieces?

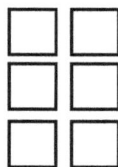

A. cone   B. cube   C. pyramid

THURSDAY Measurement

1 What is the better estimate of the temperature on hot sunny day?

A. 3°C   B. 30°C

2 The time is 1:00 p.m. What time will it be in 4 hours?

A. 5:00 p.m.

B. 5:15 p.m.

C. 5:30 p.m.

3 Find the perimeter and the area of the shaded shape.

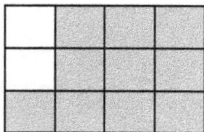

The perimeter is _____ units.

The area is _____ square units.

4 One litre of juice fills 6 cups. How many cups can you fill if you have 4 litres of juice?

Use a model to help solve the problem.

_____ cups

FRIDAY Data Management

Use the calendar to answer the questions.

September

Sunday	Monday	Tuesday	Wednesday	Thursday	Friday	Saturday
		1	2	3	4	5
6	7	8	9	10	11	12
13	14	15	16	17	18	19
20	21	22	23	24	25	26
27	28	29	30			

1 How many Wednesdays are in the month of September? _____

2 What day of the week is September 17th? _____

3 Name the date that is 5 days after September 23rd. _____

4 What date is the second Tuesday in September? _____

5 What day of the week does the month end on? _____

BRAIN STRETCH

Wendy had 24 trophies. She divided them into groups of 4.
How many groups of trophies did she have?

MONDAY — Patterning and Algebra

1 Find the missing number.

666, 665, 664, _____, 662, 661

2 Which number sentence has the same quotient as $36 \div 6$?

A. $60 \div 10$ B. $90 \div 2$ C. $48 \div 6$

3 Complete the fact family.

$4 \times 9 = 36$ ___ $\times 4 = 36$

$36 \div 9 =$ ___   ___ $\div 4 = 9$

4 Extend the pattern.

25, 50, 75, _____, _____, _____

5 Solve the equation.

$60 \div 12 =$ ___

TUESDAY — Number Sense and Operations

1 Round the following numbers to the nearest 10.

A. 39 _____

B. 55 _____

C. 94 _____

3 Count on by 100s.

3400 _____ _____ _____

5 Estimate and then solve the difference.

Estimate _____

     851
   − 289

2 $2 \times 3 \times 6 = 6 \times 6$

A. True   B. False

Show how you know.

4
     287
  + 576

Week 18

WEDNESDAY Geometry

1 Name a shape that has 3 vertices.

_____

2 Circle the shapes that look congruent.

3 How many edges?

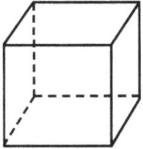

_____

4 How many lines of symmetry does this number have?

2

_____

5 Circle the shapes with 3 vertices.

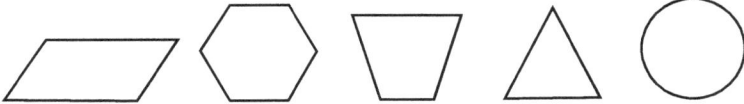

THURSDAY Measurement

1 Which distance is longer?

A. 1 metre   B. 100 kilometre

2 What is the best unit of measure for the width of a hand?

A. milimetre

B. centimetre

C. metre

3 Find the perimeter and the area of the shaded shape.

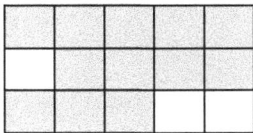

The perimeter is _____ units.

The area is _____ square units.

4 Order the temperatures from highest to lowest.

6°C, –8°C, 22°C

_____, _____, _____

FRIDAY Data Management

Use the calendar to answer the questions.

August

Sunday	Monday	Tuesday	Wednesday	Thursday	Friday	Saturday
				1	2	3
4	5	6	7	8	9	10
11	12	13	14	15	16	17
18	19	20	21	22	23	24
25	26	27	28	29	30	31

1 How many Sundays are in the month of August? _____

2 What day of the week is August 15th? _____

3 Name the date that is 1 week after August 18th. _____

4 What date is the third Tuesday in August? _____

5 What day of the week does the month end on? _____

BRAIN STRETCH

Tim has 4 bags with 6 marbles in each bag.
Simon has 5 bags with 2 marbles in each bag.
How many more marbles does Tim have than Simon?

MONDAY Patterning and Algebra

1 Find the missing number.

200 400 600 _____ 1000

2 Which number sentence has the same sum as 22 + 8?

A. 11 + 11   B. 15 + 15   C. 10 + 10

3 Fill in the blank to make the equation true.

$5 \times 2 = 5 +$ _____

4 Solve the equation.

$63 = 9 \times$ _____

5 What is the next number if the pattern rule is subtract 12?

54, _____

TUESDAY Number Sense and Operations

1 Write the numbers in expanded form.

A. 531 _____

B. 214 _____

2 Compare the numbers using <, >, or =.

945 ☐ 945

3 Count on by 1s.

857, _____, _____, _____, _____

4 Write each amount in decimal form.

A. four dollars and fourteen cents

_____

B. eighty-two cents

_____

5 Circle $\frac{1}{3}$ of the group.

WEDNESDAY Geometry

1 What shape does this sign look like?

_____

2 Is this shape a quadrilateral?

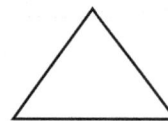

A. yes
B. no

3 How many faces?

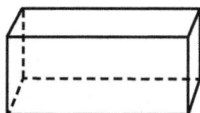

_____

4 How many lines of symmetry?

J _____

5 What 3D shape could be made from these pieces?

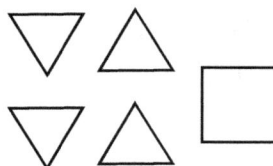

A. cone   B. cube   C. pyramid

THURSDAY Measurement

1 Find the perimeter and the area of the shaded shape.

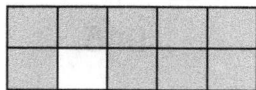

The perimeter is _____ units.

The area is _____ square units.

3 Order the temperatures from highest to lowest.

15°C, –5°C, 30°C

_____, _____, _____

2

What time is it? _____

What time was it 30 minutes ago? _____

4 What is the best unit of measure for the width of a house?

A. cm   B. m   C. km

FRIDAY Data Management

Ms. Robinson conducted a class survey on favourite recess activities. Read the graph and answer the questions.

Favourite Recess Activities

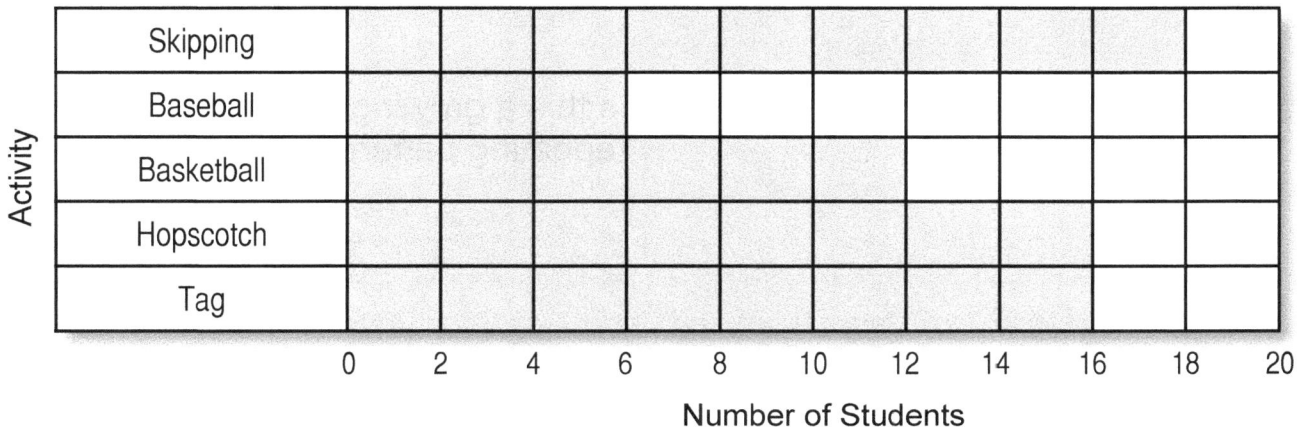

Activity											
Skipping											
Baseball											
Basketball											
Hopscotch											
Tag											

0　2　4　6　8　10　12　14　16　18　20

Number of Students

1 The most popular recess activity is _____.

2 Which two activities had the same number of votes? _____

3 Which activity had 6 votes? _____

4 List the recess activities from least popular to most popular.

_____

BRAIN STRETCH

Ms. Poulos wanted to buy cookies for her class. Each box had 6 cookies. How many boxes of cookies did she need if she had 24 students in her class?

MONDAY — Patterning and Algebra

1 Find the missing number.

29, 39, 49, _____, 69, 79

2 Which number sentence has the same answer as 30 − 9?

A. 16 + 2   B. 18 + 3   C. 10 + 1

3 Solve the equation.

70 ÷ _____ = 10

4 Is this a growing, shrinking, or repeating pattern?

5 What is the next number if the pattern rule is add 20?

20, _____

_____

TUESDAY — Number Sense and Operations

1 Draw three coins to show 55¢.

2 Round the numbers to the nearest 10.

A. 165 _____

B. 722 _____

3 Count on by 25s.

100, _____, _____, _____, _____

4 Estimate and then solve the difference.

$$\begin{array}{r} 671 \\ -\ 478 \end{array}$$

Estimate _____

5 Order the numbers from greatest to least.

321   244   638   12

_____ > _____ > _____ > _____

WEDNESDAY Geometry

1 What shape does this sign look like?

_____

3 How many edges?

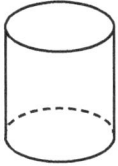

_____

2 Look at the shapes. Choose flip, slide, or turn.

A. flip   B. slide   C. turn

4 How many right angles does an octagon have?

_____

5 Circle the shapes with 2 pairs of parallel sides.

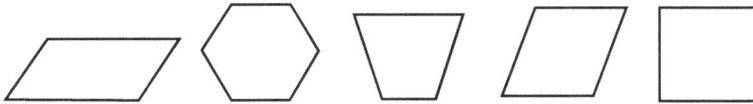

THURSDAY Measurement

1 The time is 7:30 p.m.
What time was it 2 hours ago?

A. 5:00 p.m.

B. 5:15 p.m.

C. 5:30 p.m.

3 Find the perimeter and the area of the shaded shape.

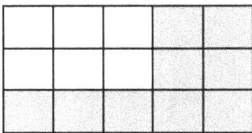

The perimeter is _____ units.

The area is _____ square units.

2 What time is it?

_____

4 Show how to divide the shape in question #3 into 2 rectangles.

Find the area of each rectangle.

Add to find the total area.

Ms. Robinson conducted a class survey on favourite juice.
Read the graph and answer the questions.

Favourite Juice

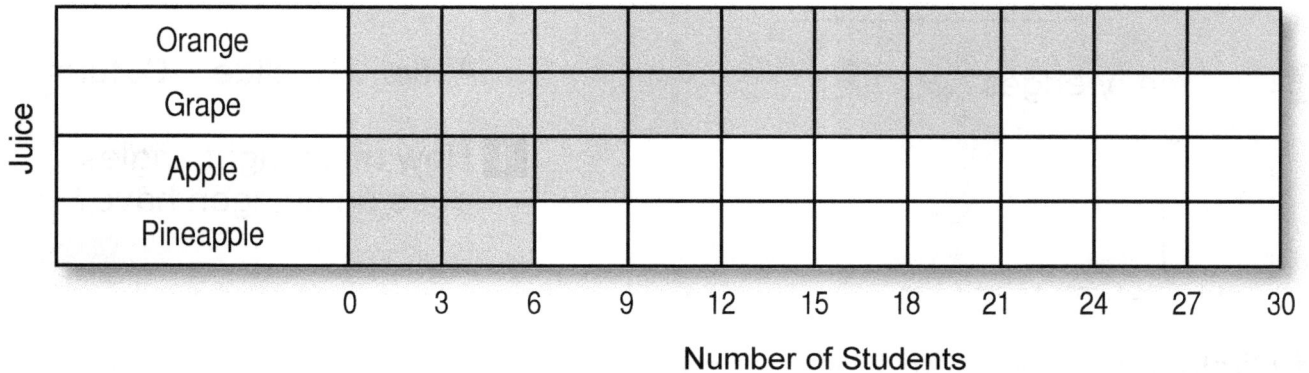

Juice											
Orange											
Grape											
Apple											
Pineapple											

0   3   6   9   12   15   18   21   24   27   30

Number of Students

1 How many people chose either grape or apple? _____

2 The least popular juice is _____.

3 List the juices from least popular to most popular.

_____

4 How many more people liked orange than liked pineapple? _____

Patricia has 1 red hair ribbon and 2 blue hair ribbons.
What fraction of Patricia's hair ribbons are blue?

MONDAY Patterning and Algebra

1 Find the missing number.

75, 80, 85, _____, 95, 100

2 Which number sentence has the same quotient as 48 ÷ 6?

A. 32 ÷ 8   B. 64 ÷ 8   C. 40 ÷ 8

3 Ruby rides her bike 3 km a day. She plans to ride a total of 30 km. After 7 days, how many more km does she have left to ride? Write an equation and solve.

4 Write two multiplication sentences for the array.

OOOOOOOOO
OOOOOOOOO
OOOOOOOOO

_____ × _____ = _____

_____ × _____ = _____

TUESDAY Number Sense and Operations

1 80 × 9 =

2 Count back by 1s.

675, _____, _____, _____, _____

3 Write the number word for 888.

_____

4 Round the numbers to the nearest 10.

A. 21 _____

B. 66 _____

5 What is the value of the coins?

_____

6 Compare the two fractions. Choose > or <.

$\dfrac{3}{5}$ ☐ $\dfrac{2}{5}$

WEDNESDAY Geometry

1 What shape does this sign look like?

STOP

_____

2 Turn this shape.

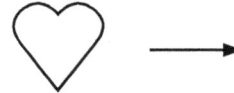

3 How many faces?

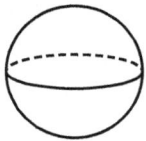

_____

4 Circle the polygons with 4 vertices.

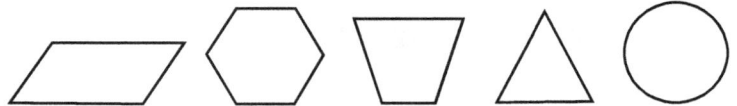

THURSDAY Measurement

1 What time is it?

_____

3 Which tool would you use to measure the flour in a cake recipe?

A. scale

B. thermometre

C. measuring cup

2 Find the perimeter and the area of the shaded shape.

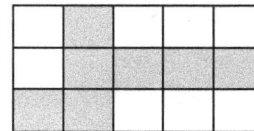

The perimeter is _____ units.

The area is _____ square units.

4 The time is 4:30 p.m. What time will it be in 20 minutes?

A. 5:00 p.m.

B. 4:50 p.m.

C. 4:30 p.m.

Week 21

FRIDAY Data Management

Mrs. Turnbull conducted a survey on students' favourite places to visit.
Use the information from the bar graph to answer the questions.

Favourite Places To Visit

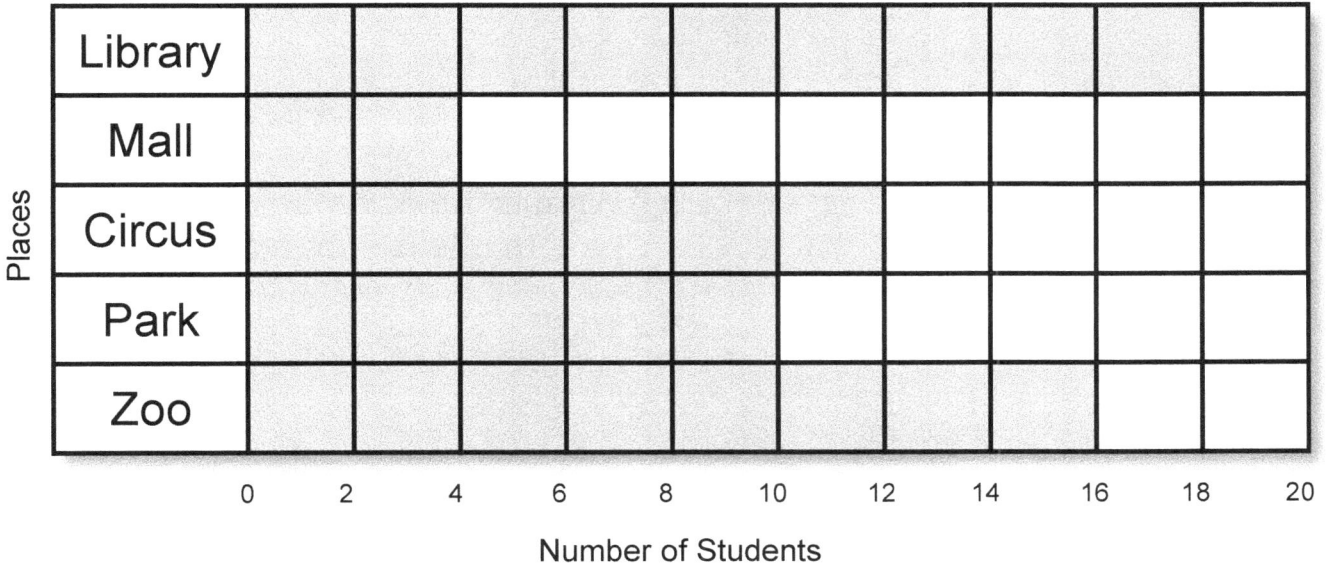

Places										
Library										
Mall										
Circus										
Park										
Zoo										

0   2   4   6   8   10   12   14   16   18   20

Number of Students

1 How many fewer students chose the mall than chose the zoo? _____

2 How many students chose the zoo? _____

3 What is the least popular place to visit? _____

4 What is the most popular place to visit? _____

5 List the favourite places in order from most popular to least popular.

_____

BRAIN STRETCH

Bill's family drinks 3 L of orange juice a day.
How many litres of orange juice will Bill's family drink in a week?

MONDAY Patterning and Algebra

1 Find the missing number.

67, 69, 71, _____, 75, 77, 79

2 Which number sentence has the same product as 10×4?

A. 6×8 B. 5×8 C. 4×8

3 Find the missing factor.

$4 \times h = 20$

$h = $ _____

4 What is the next number if the pattern rule is subtract 30?

100, _____

TUESDAY Number Sense and Operations

1 $25 \div 5 = $

2 $3 \times 50 = $

3 Write the numeral for:

$200 + 10 + 6$

_____

4 What is the number?

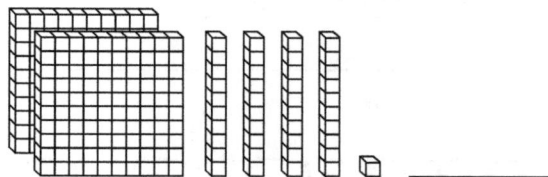

_____

5 What fraction does the number line show? _____

WEDNESDAY Geometry

1 What 3D shape does the fruit look like?

_____

2 Circle a set of perpendicular lines.

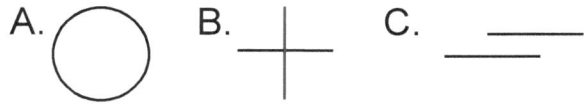

A. ◯ B. + C. ____

3 How many edges?

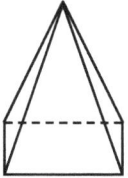

_____

4 How many lines of symmetry does this letter have?

A _____

5 What 3D shape could be made from these pieces?

A. cone   B. cylinder   C. pyramid

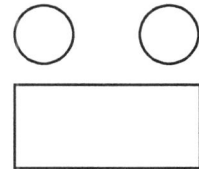

THURSDAY Measurement

1 What time is it?

_____

2 Order the temperatures from highest to lowest.

8°C, 29°C, −10°C

_____, _____, _____

3 Find the perimeter of the triangle.

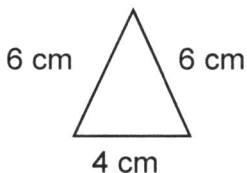

6 cm   6 cm

4 cm

_____

4 What is the area of the shaded shape?

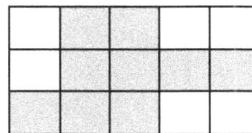

_____ square units

FRIDAY Data Management

Mr. Lopez's class conducted a survey on favourite seasons.
Add the missing labels to the graph.
Complete the graph and answer the questions.

Favourite Season

Season	Number of Votes
Spring	35
Summer	50
Autumn	40
Winter	20

Favourite Season Graph

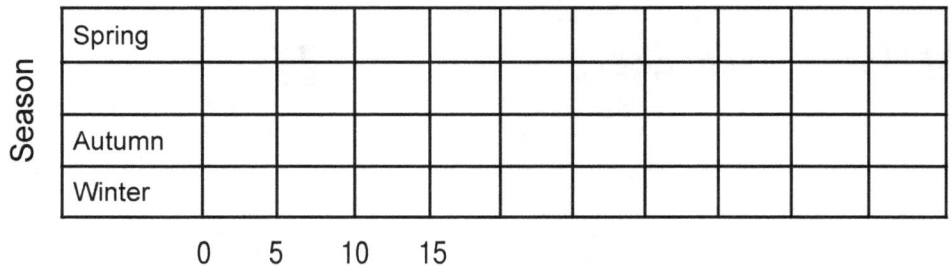

Season

Spring										
Autumn										
Winter										

0   5   10   15

_____

1 How many people chose either summer or winter? _____

2 What is the most popular season? _____

3 List the seasons from the most popular to the least popular.

_____

4 How many more people liked autumn than liked spring? _____

BRAIN STRETCH

How are the attributes of a rectangle and a square the same?

MONDAY Patterning and Algebra

1 Find the missing number.

781, 780, 779, _____, 777, 776

2 Which number sentence has the same sum as 8 + 8?

A. 6 + 2   B. 8 + 4   C. 10 + 6

4 What letter comes next?

G G U P G G U P G G U P _____

3 What is the next number if the pattern rule is add 11?

50, _____

TUESDAY Number Sense and Operations

1 Write each amount in decimal form.

A. seven dollars
   and fifty cents _____

B. ninety cents _____

2 Round the following numbers to the nearest 10.

A. 35 _____

B. 62 _____

3 8 × 7 =

4 Find the missing number.

300 + _____ + 1 = 381

5 What fraction does the number line show? _____

WEDNESDAY Geometry

1 Flip this shape.

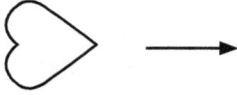

2 What shape does the pool table look like?

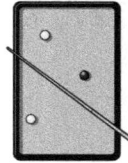

_____

3 Circle the pair of shapes that look congruent.

4 How many vertices?

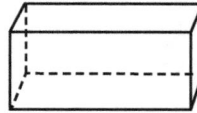

_____

5 Circle the shapes that are not quadrilaterals.

THURSDAY Measurement

1 The time is 10:00 a.m. What time will it be in 30 minutes?

A. 10:00 a.m.

B. 10:15 a.m.

C. 10:30 a.m.

2 Draw a line 4 cm long.

3 Find the perimeter and the area of the shaded shape.

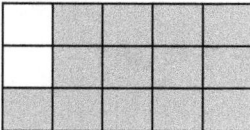

The perimeter is _____ units.

The area is _____ square units.

4 What time is it?

_____

The third grade classes conducted a survey on their favourite games.
They displayed the data as a pictograph.
Use the pictograph to answer the questions.

Favourite Video Game

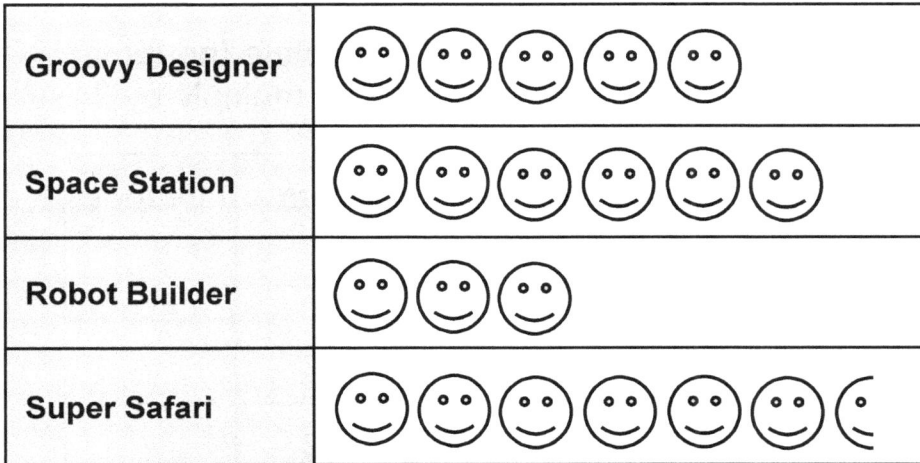

Groovy Designer	☺ ☺ ☺ ☺ ☺
Space Station	☺ ☺ ☺ ☺ ☺ ☺
Robot Builder	☺ ☺ ☺
Super Safari	☺ ☺ ☺ ☺ ☺ ☺ ☺

Key: ☺ = 4 Students

1 How many students chose Super Safari? _____

2 How many more students chose Space Station than chose Robot Builder?

_____

3 How many students chose Groovy Designer or Robot Builder? _____

4 How many students were surveyed? _____

BRAIN STRETCH

How are the attributes of a parallelogram and a triangle different?

MONDAY Patterning and Algebra

1 Find the missing number.

16, 24, 32, _____, 48, 56, 64

2 Which number sentence has the same quotient as $50 \div 5$?

A. $80 \div 8$ B. $60 \div 10$ C. $40 \div 10$

3 What is the missing number?

$8 \times$ _____ $= 80$

4 Complete the table.
Rule: multiply by 2.

Input	Output
6	
3	
10	

5 Gina collects stamps. She got 123 stamps in the first month, 43 stamps in the second month, and 91 stamps in the third month.

Estimate the total number of stamps. Show your work.

Add to find the total stamps.

TUESDAY Number Sense and Operations

1 $72 \div 9 =$

2 Write the numeral for eight hundred eleven. _____

3 Are these numbers even or odd?

A. 99 _____

B. 44 _____

4 Show $\frac{3}{4}$ on the number line.

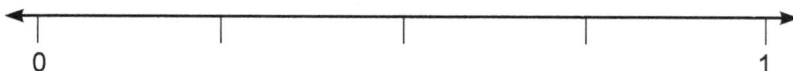

0   1

5 Colour each shape to show the fraction. $\frac{2}{9}$ 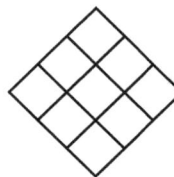 $\frac{5}{9}$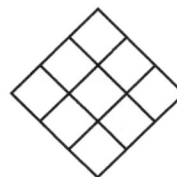

© Chalkboard Publishing

WEDNESDAY Geometry

1 What shape does the refrigerator look like?

_____

2 Which of the following is a ray?

A. ←————————→

B. •————————→

C. •————————•

D. •

3 How many vertices?

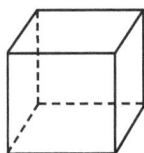

_____

4 Draw a line of symmetry.

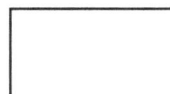

5 Circle the shapes that have 2 pairs of parallel sides.

THURSDAY Measurement

1 The time is 9:00 p.m. What time will it be in 15 minutes?

A. 9:00 p.m.

B. 9:15 p.m.

C. 9:30 p.m.

2 Which measuring tool would you use to weigh a person?

A. scale   B. ruler   C. calendar

3 Find the perimeter and the area of the shaded shape.

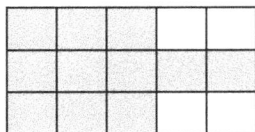

The perimeter is _____ units.

The area is _____ square units.

4 What time is it?

_____

FRIDAY   Data Management

Use the calendar to answer the questions.

November

Sunday	Monday	Tuesday	Wednesday	Thursday	Friday	Saturday
				1	2	3
4	5	6	7	8	9	10
11	12	13	14	15	16	17
18	19	20	21	22	23	24
25	26	27	28	29	30	

1 How many Mondays are in the month of November? _____

2 What day of the week is November 5th? _____

3 Name the date that is 2 weeks after November 3rd. _____

4 What is the date of the third Sunday in November? _____

5 What day of the week does the month end on? _____

BRAIN STRETCH

Write 6 subtraction facts that have an answer of 5.

Week 24

MONDAY Patterning and Algebra

1 Find the missing number.

455, 465, 475, _____, 495

2 Is this a growing, shrinking, or repeating pattern?

1, 5, 1, 5, 1, 5, 1, 5

_____

3 Find the missing factor and quotient.

6 × _____ = 42   42 ÷ 7 = _____

4 Complete the table.
Rule: divide by 3.

Input	Output
18	
24	
9	

TUESDAY Number Sense and Operations

1 Estimate and then solve the sum.

          562
Estimate _____   + 178

2 Write the numeral in standard form.

900 + 40 + 3 = _____

3 What number is 10 less than 54?

_____

4 20 ÷ 2 =

5 Compare the two fractions. Choose > or <.

$\frac{3}{4}$ ☐ $\frac{1}{4}$

6 Write an addition sentence that equals 3 × 9. Include the sum.

WEDNESDAY   Geometry

1 Draw a triangle with a right angle.

2 Slide this shape.

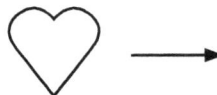

3 How many faces?

_____

4 Which shape does not have a line of symmetry?

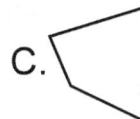

A.   B.   C.

5 What 3D shape could be made from these pieces?

A. cone   B. cylinder   C. rectangular prism

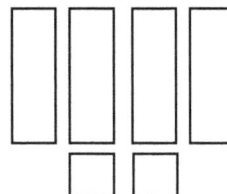

THURSDAY   Measurement

1 The time is 11:00 a.m. What time was it 45 minutes ago?

A. 10:00 a.m.

B. 10:15 a.m.

C. 10:30 a.m.

2 Which measuring tool would you use to weigh some apples?

A. scale   B. ruler   C. calendar

3 Find the perimeter and the area of the shaded shape.

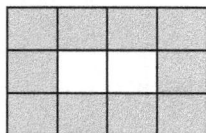

The perimeter is _____ units.

The area is _____ square units.

4 What time is it?

_____

Week 25

FRIDAY Data Management

Use the calendar to answer the questions.

April

Sunday	Monday	Tuesday	Wednesday	Thursday	Friday	Saturday
					1	2
3	4	5	6	7	8	9
10	11	12	13	14	15	16
17	18	19	20	21	22	23
24	25	26	27	28	29	30

1 What day of the week is April 18th? _____

2 How many Saturdays are there in this month? _____

3 On what day of the week will the next month begin? _____

4 What is the date of the second Thursday? _____

5 What is the date of the first Tuesday? _____

BRAIN STRETCH

1 5 × 10 =

2 4 × 9 =

3 5 × 6 =

4 81 ÷ 9 =

5 3 × 3 =

6 16 ÷ 2 =

7 3 × 8 =

8 49 ÷ 7 =

9 90 ÷ 9 =

10 21 ÷ 3 =

11 6 ÷ 6 =

12 7 × 8 =

MONDAY — Patterning and Algebra

1 Find the missing number.

33, 43, 53, _____, 73, 83

2 Which number sentence has the same quotient as 45 ÷ 5?

A. 65 ÷ 8   B. 90 ÷ 10   C. 24 ÷ 6

3 Compare using <, >, or =.

8 × 3 ☐ 30

4 Complete the table.
Rule: subtract 9.

Input	Output
89	
40	
28	

5 What is the pattern rule?

10, 20, 40, 80

_____

TUESDAY — Number Sense and Operations

1 6 × 40 =

2 Bessie put two roses and five lilies into a vase. What fraction of Bessie's flowers are roses?

3 Fill in the missing number to make two equivalent fractions.

$\dfrac{}{4} = \dfrac{6}{8}$

$\frac{1}{4}$		$\frac{1}{4}$		$\frac{1}{4}$		
$\frac{1}{8}$	$\frac{1}{8}$	$\frac{1}{8}$	$\frac{1}{8}$	$\frac{1}{8}$	$\frac{1}{8}$	

4 Round the following numbers to the nearest 10.

A. 23 _____

B. 47 _____

Week 26

WEDNESDAY Geometry

1 Draw a set of intersecting lines.

2 Choose the word that best describes this shape.

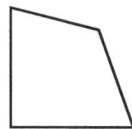

A. quadrilateral

B. square

C. rectangle

3 How many vertices?

_____

4 Circle the shapes that look congruent.

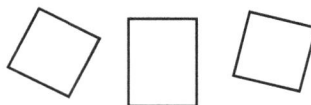

5 Circle the shapes that have 4 sides and 4 right angles.

THURSDAY Measurement

1 What time is it?

_____

2 The time is 6:30 p.m. What time was it 30 minutes ago?

A. 6:00 p.m.

B. 5:45 p.m.

C. 5:30 p.m.

3 What is the perimeter?

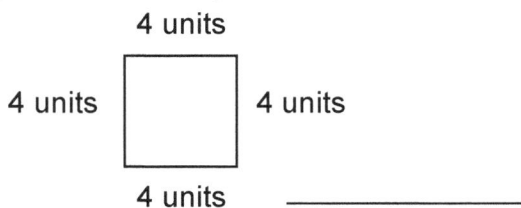

4 units

4 units   4 units

4 units   _____

4 What is the area of the shaded shape?

_____ square units

5 Which measuring tool would you use for an amount of milk?

A. scale   B. ruler   C. measuring cup

The students in Ms. Chang's class voted for the types of presents they like to receive. This bar graph shows the results. Answer the questions using information from the graph.

Presents Students Like to Receive

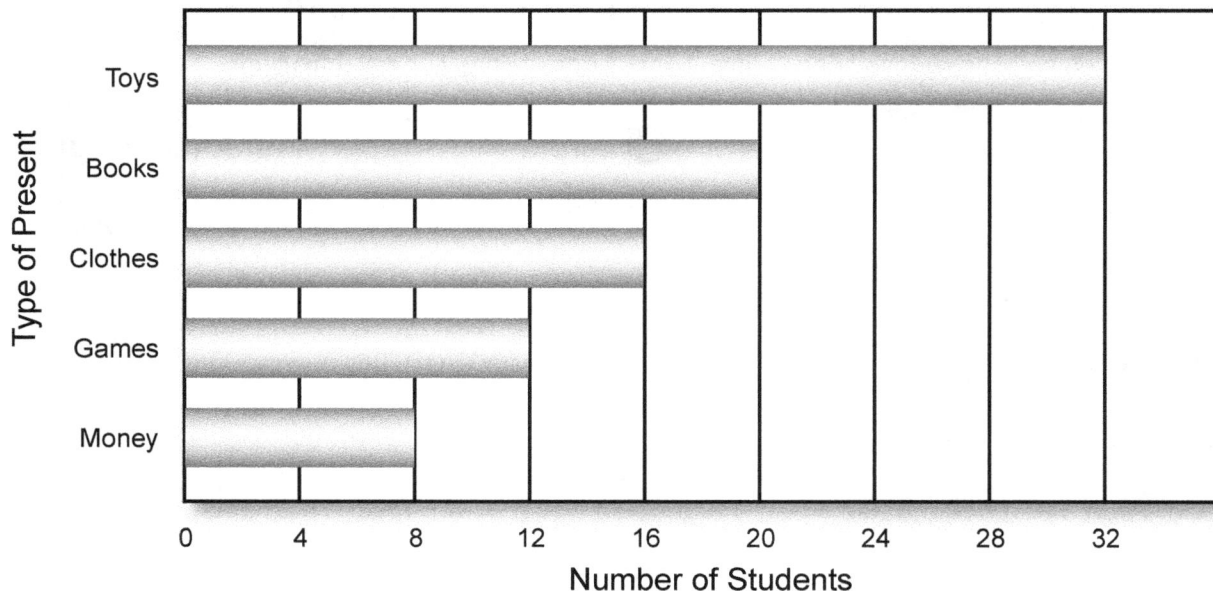

Type of Present: Toys, Books, Clothes, Games, Money

Number of Students (scale: 0, 4, 8, 12, 16, 20, 24, 28, 32)

1 What interval was used for this scale? _____

2 How many more students voted for books than for money?_____

3 Which type of present received 16 votes?_____

4 How many fewer students voted for games than for clothes?_____

BRAIN STRETCH

1 5 × 7 =   **2** 2 × 7 =   **3** 9 × 9 =

4 30 ÷ 6 =   **5** 8 × 9 =   **6** 20 ÷ 2 =

7 6 × 6 =   **8** 70 ÷ 7 =   **9** 100 ÷ 10 =

10 14 ÷ 2 =   **11** 45 ÷ 9 =   **12** 4 × 9 =

MONDAY Patterning and Algebra

1 Find the missing number.

73, 78, 83, _____, 93, 98

2 Which number sentence has the same product as 6 × 6?

A. 4 × 9   B. 3 × 9   C. 2 × 9

3 Find the missing factor.

$9 \times h = 72$

$h =$ _____

4 Complete the table.
Rule: subtract 100.

Input	Output
311	
567	
185	

5 Extend the pattern.

88, 86, 84, _____, _____, _____

TUESDAY Number Sense and Operations

1 Estimate and then solve the sum.

```
      236
    + 397
```
Estimate _____

2 Write the numerals in standard form.

A. 800 + 20 + 1 = _____

B. 400 + 30 + 7 = _____

3 Count on by 25s.

750, _____, _____, _____, _____

4 What is the number?

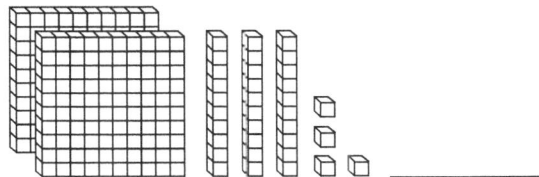

_____

5 Compare the two fractions.
Choose > or <.

$\frac{1}{4}$ ☐ $\frac{1}{8}$

WEDNESDAY Geometry

1 Name an object that looks like a cylinder.

_____

2 Flip this shape.

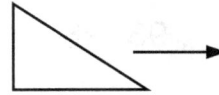

3 What shape is on the top of a cylinder?

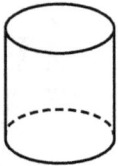

_____

4 Draw a line of symmetry.

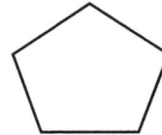

5 What 3D shape could be made from these pieces?

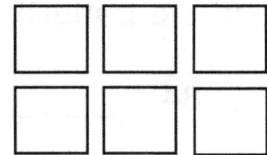

A. pyramid   B. cylinder   C. cube

THURSDAY Measurement

1 How many months in 3 years?

_____

2 What time will it be 4 hours from now?

_____

3 What is the area of the shaded shape?

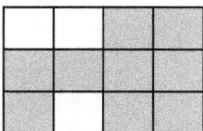

_____ square units

4 What is the perimeter of the rectangle? _____

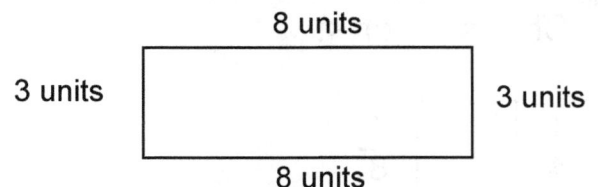

8 units

3 units   3 units

8 units

5 How many metres in a kilometre?

_____

FRIDAY Data Management

Mei Ling conducted a class survey on favourite book genres. Use the results from her survey to create a bar graph and answer the questions.

_____

Favourite Book Genre

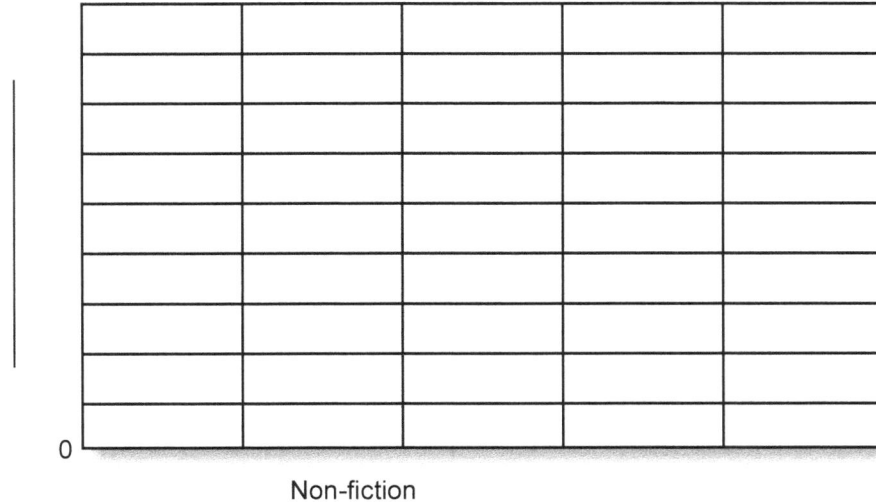

Book Genre	Tally
Mystery	⊦⊦⊦ ⊦⊦⊦ ‖
Non-fiction	⊦⊦⊦ ‖‖
Fiction	⊦⊦⊦ ‖‖
Biography	⊦⊦⊦ ⊦⊦⊦ ⊦⊦⊦
Adventure	‖‖‖

0

Non-fiction

_____

1 Which book genre was the most popular? _____

2 List the book genres from the most popular to the least popular.

_____

3 Which interval did you use for the scale? _____

4 About how many books in all genres were read? _____

5 What book genre would you buy as a gift for the library? Explain why.

_____

BRAIN STRETCH

Stephen went to the store and bought a drink and snack for $4.55. He paid with a $5.00 bill. What was Stephen's change?

MONDAY · Patterning and Algebra

1 Find the missing number.

100, 150, 200, _____, 300, 350

2 Which number sentence has the same quotient as 54 ÷ 6?

A. 14 ÷ 7   B. 70 ÷ 10   C. 18 ÷ 2

3 Complete the fact family.

8 × 10 = 80   ___ × 8 = 80

80 ÷ 8 = ___   ___ ÷ 10 = 8

4 What is the rule?

Input	Output
69	59
124	114
15	5

A. add 10

B. subtract 10

C. multiply by 2

5 What is the next number if the pattern rule is subtract 12?

76, _____

TUESDAY · Number Sense and Operations

1
```
    592
  − 215
```

2 Round the following numbers to the nearest 100.

A. 173 _____

B. 562 _____

C. 450 _____

3 Stephen read 3 non-fiction books and 5 fiction books in one week. What fraction of the books read by Stephen were fiction?

4 10 × 3 < 6 × 2 × 3

A. True   B. False

5 Circle $\frac{5}{6}$ of the group.

WEDNESDAY Geometry

1 Name an object that looks like a cone.

_____

2 Does this picture show a line of symmetry?

A. yes

B. no

3 How many faces?

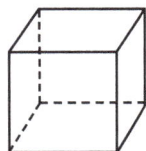

_____

4 What shape can these two triangles make when combined?

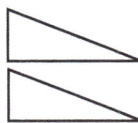

A. rhombus
B. rectangle
C. trapezoid

5 Circle the shapes that have 4 right angles and 4 equal sides.

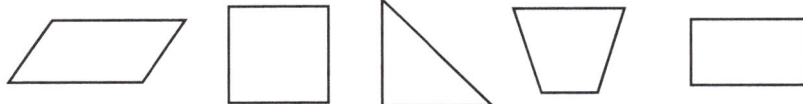

THURSDAY Measurement

1 Calculate the area of the rectangle. _____

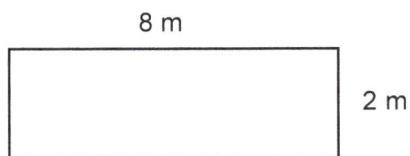

8 m

2 m

2 What time is it?

_____

3 The perimeter of the rectangle is 140 units. What is the length of the unknown side? _____ units

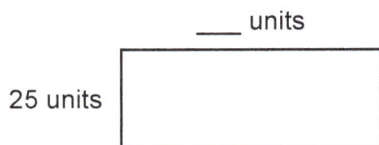

___ units

25 units

4 What is the perimeter of the shaded shape?

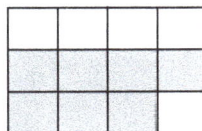

_____ units

The third grade classes took a survey of their personal collections. They displayed the data as a pictograph. Use the pictograph to answer the questions.

Types of Collections

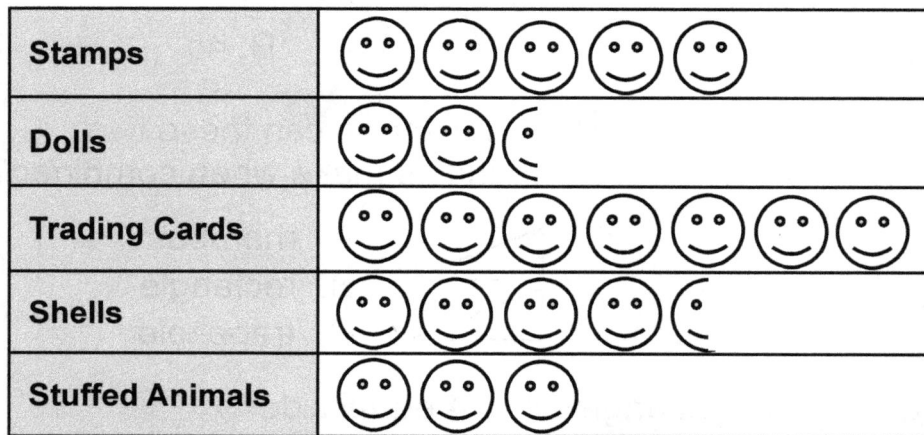

Stamps	☺ ☺ ☺ ☺ ☺
Dolls	☺ ☺ (
Trading Cards	☺ ☺ ☺ ☺ ☺ ☺ ☺
Shells	☺ ☺ ☺ ☺ (
Stuffed Animals	☺ ☺ ☺

Key: ☺ = 4 Students

1 How many students have a shell collection? _____

2 How many more students collect trading cards than collect stuffed animals? _____

3 Which type of collection is the most popular? _____

4 How many students collect dolls or stamps? _____

5 How many students have a stamp collection? _____

BRAIN STRETCH

1 5 × 8 =

2 3 × 7 =

3 1 × 10 =

4 25 ÷ 5 =

5 10 × 9 =

6 60 ÷ 6 =

7 7 × 6 =

8 24 ÷ 8 =

9 9 ÷ 3 =

10 18 ÷ 2 =

11 63 ÷ 9 =

12 4 × 2 =

MONDAY — Patterning and Algebra

1 Find the missing number.

225, 250, 275, _____, 325, 350

2 Choose a number to make the number sentence correct.

$6 + 4 + 7 = 3 + \underline{\hphantom{00}} + 9$

A. 4   B. 5   C. 10

3 Complete the fact family.

$5 \times 7 = 35$ $\underline{\hphantom{00}} \times 5 = 35$

$35 \div 5 = \underline{\hphantom{00}}$ $\underline{\hphantom{00}} \div 7 = 5$

4 Complete the table. Rule: add 100.

Input	Output
777	
89	
103	

5 What is the pattern rule?

34, 31, 28, 25, 22

_____

TUESDAY — Number Sense and Operations

1 Estimate and then solve the difference.

Estimate _____

$\begin{array}{r} 540 \\ -\ 365 \\ \hline \end{array}$

2 What is 100 more than 533?

_____

3 $32 \div 8 =$

4 $2 \times 3 \times 4 = 3 \times 4 \times 2$

A. True   B. False

Show how you know.

5 Fill in the missing number to make two equivalent fractions.

$\dfrac{1}{2} = \dfrac{}{6}$

$\frac{1}{6}$	$\frac{1}{6}$	$\frac{1}{6}$			
$\frac{1}{2}$					

6 $7 \times 40 =$

WEDNESDAY Geometry

1 Name an object that looks like a cube.

_____

3 How many edges?

_____

5 Circle the shapes that have parallel sides.

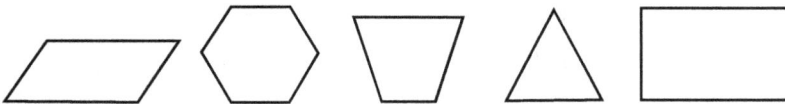

2 Draw a square and a rectangle.

A. How are they alike?

_____

B. How are they different?

_____

4 Does this picture show a line of symmetry?

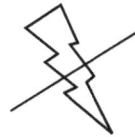

A. yes

B. no

THURSDAY Measurement

1 How many days in 7 weeks?

_____

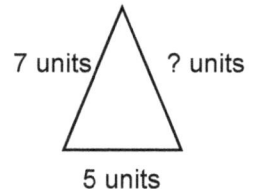

3 What is the area of the shaded shape?

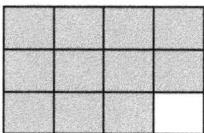

_____ square units

5 How many minutes between 2:00 and 5:00?

_____

2 If the perimeter of the triangle is 20 units, what is the length of the unknown side?

_____ units

7 units ? units

5 units

4 Calculate the perimeter of the hexagon.

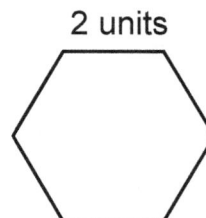

2 units

_____ units

© Chalkboard Publishing

Finish the bar graph to display the information from the chart.
Write two sentences about what you can conclude from the graph.

Favourite School Subjects

Subject	Tally
Reading	35
Art	25
Math	15
Science	10
Music	20

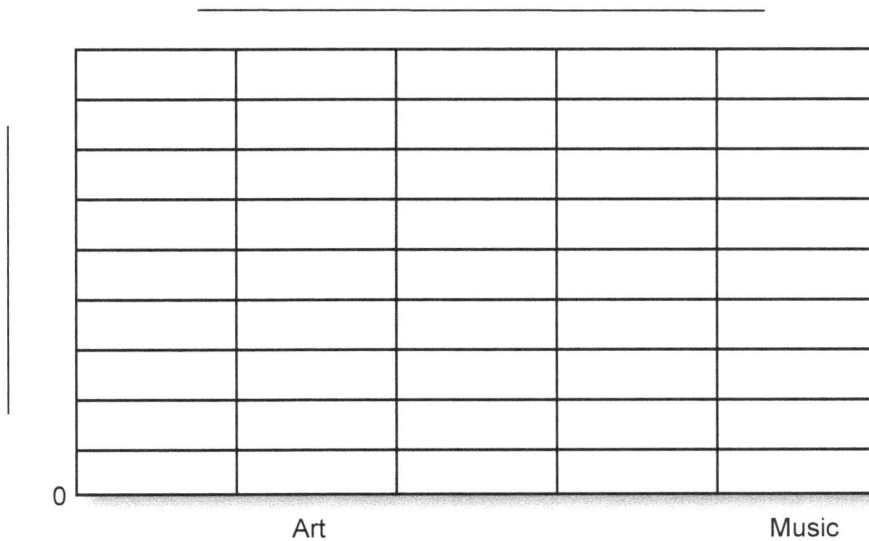

_____

0

Art   Music

_____

_____

_____

_____

BRAIN STRETCH

Alex reads 3 pages of a book on Monday, 6 pages of a book Tuesday, 9 pages of a book Wednesday. If Alex continues his reading pattern, how many pages of a book will he read on Friday?

MONDAY — Patterning and Algebra

1 Find the missing number.

88, 78, 68, _____, 48, 38

2 Which number sentence has the same product as 4 × 5?

A. 6 × 3   B. 10 × 2   C. 7 × 2

3 Find the missing factor and quotient.

4 × _____ = 20   20 ÷ 4 = _____

4 What is the rule?

Input	Output
5	10
7	14
10	20

A. add 10

B. subtract 10

C. multiply by 2

5 Is this a growing, shrinking, or repeating pattern?

_____

TUESDAY — Number Sense and Operations

1 Estimate and then solve the difference.

Estimate _____
```
  872
- 169
```

3 Write each amount in decimal form.

A. nine dollars _____

B. seventy-five cents _____

4 Circle $\frac{1}{4}$ of the group.

2 There are 166 jelly beans in one bag and 181 in another bag. Dana estimated to the nearest 10 before finding the total. Nathan estimated to the nearest 100 before adding.

A. What was each total?

Dana: _____ Nathan: _____

B. Add to find the total:

166 + 181 = _____

Whose estimate was closer?

_____

WEDNESDAY Geometry

1 Draw a set of parallel lines.

2 Draw a square and a rhombus.

A. How are they alike?

_____

B. How are they different?

_____

3 Which pair of shapes look congruent?

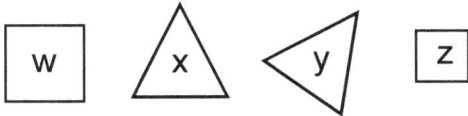

w   x   y   z

A. w and x   B. x and y   C. w and z

4 Circle the shapes that have 2 pairs of parallel sides.

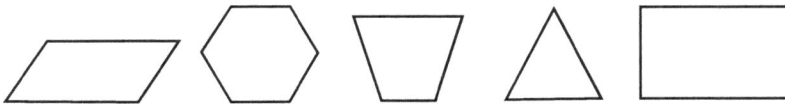

THURSDAY Measurement

1 Draw a line $1\frac{1}{2}$ cm long.

2 Jason gets home from school at 3:45. It takes 10 minutes to eat a snack, 20 minutes to play piano, and 15 minutes to do homework. Use the number line to help find what time he can go outside.

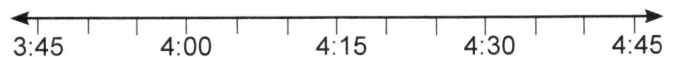

3:45   4:00   4:15   4:30   4:45

3 Show two ways to find the area of the shaded shape.

A. Count.
B. Divide into smaller shapes.

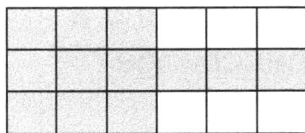

_____ square units

4 Calculate the perimeter of the rectangle.   _____ metres

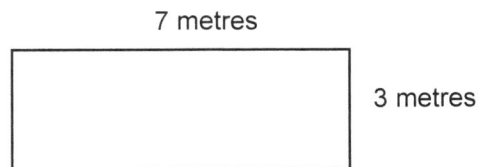

7 metres

3 metres

© Chalkboard Publishing

Finish the bar graph to display the information from the chart.
Write two sentences about what you can conclude from the graph

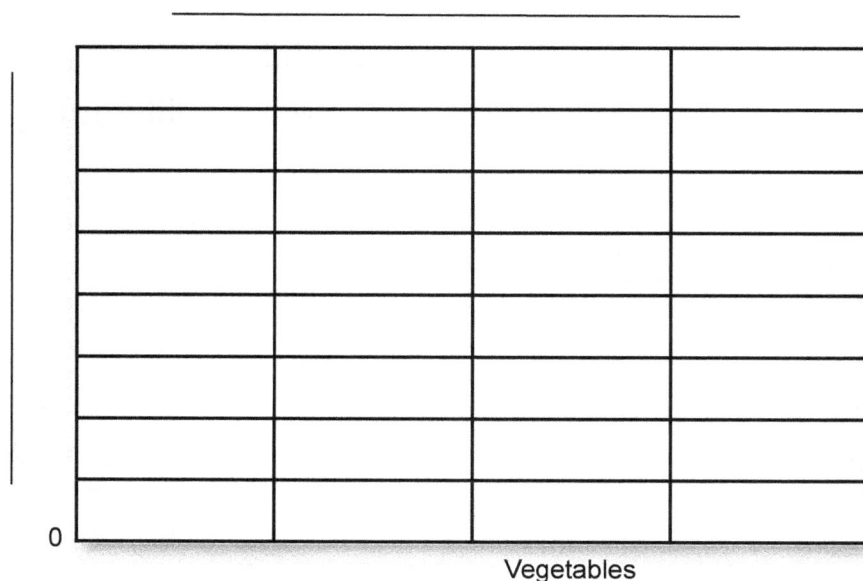

_____

0

Vegetables

_____

Favourite Pizza Toppings

Topping	Tally
Cheese	25
Pepperoni	15
Vegetables	35
Other	20

_____

_____

_____

_____

BRAIN STRETCH

Michelle went to the store and bought special markers for $2.30 and a notepad for $1.00. She paid with a $5.00 bill. What was her change?

Week 30

Math — Show What You Know!

_____

☐ I read the question and I know what I need to find.

☐ I drew a picture or a diagram to help solve the question.

☐ I showed all the steps in solving the question.

☐ I used math language to explain my thinking.

Student Tracking Sheet

Student	Week 1	Week 2	Week 3	Week 4	Week 5	Week 6	Week 7	Week 8	Week 9	Week 10	Week 11	Week 12	Week 13	Week 14	Week 15

Student Tracking Sheet

Student	Week 16	Week 17	Week 18	Week 19	Week 20	Week 21	Week 22	Week 23	Week 24	Week 25	Week 26	Week 27	Week 28	Week 29	Week 30

You Are Incredible!

Keep Up the Good Work!

_____

Week 1, pages 1–3

Monday   **1.** 12   **2.** Picture should show 3 groups of 4 crayons. 12; 3 × 4   **3.** 7   **4.** 21
5. 40, 50, 60; The terms increase by 10.

Tuesday   **1.** 830   **2.** 47   **3. A.** 70 **B.** 30   **4.** 421   **5.** $4.15

Wednesday   **1.** triangle   **2.** 4   **3.** cylinder   **4.** Accept any line that divides the circle in two equal halves.   **5.** ⬡

Thursday   **1.** 4:45   **2.** 12 units, 7 square units   **3.** C; C is 12 square units, which is greater than the area of A (3 units²) and B (8 units²).   **4.** C

Friday   The number column of the favourite colour chart should contain 7 for red, 13 for blue, 4 for green, and 7 for purple.   **1.** blue   **2.** green   **3.** 11   **4.** 31   **5.** red and purple

Brain Stretch   76 beads

Week 2, pages 4–6

Monday   **1.** 6   **2.** C   **3.** 8   **4.** 40; Arrays should show 8 groups of 5 circles each. Sample answer: 8 packages of markers each containing 5 markers   **5.** 140, 150, 160

Tuesday   **1.** 44   **2.** 932   **3. A.** 80 **B.** 40   **4.** C   **5.** Sample answer: 4 + 4 + 4 + 4 = 16

Wednesday   **1.** A   **2.** 8   **3.** cube   **4.** ✳   **5.** ▭

Thursday   **1.** 6:45 or quarter to 7   **2.** B   **3.** 16 units, 11 square units   **4.** C

Friday   **1.** breakfast ‖, lunch ‖‖, dinner ⊞‖   **2.** dinner   **3.** breakfast   **4.** 11

Brain Stretch   **1.** 89   **2.** 44   **3.** 99   **4.** 20

Week 3, pages 7–9

Monday   **1.** 24   **2.** C   **3.** 24; Arrays should show 6 groups of 4 circles each.   **4.** 44, 55

Tuesday   **1.** 402   **2. A.** 300 + 90 + 8 **B.** 600 + 50 + 1   **3. A.** 900 **B.** 2   **4.** <

Wednesday   **1.** A   **2.** cone   **3.** 1   **4.** 3   **5.** B

Thursday   **1.** B   **2.** B   **3.** 12 units, 7 square units   **4.** C

Friday   **1.** 30   **2.** orange juice   **3.** Lemonade and milk   **4.** 6

Brain Stretch   **1.** 82   **2.** 66   **3.** 91   **4.** 35

Week 4, pages 10–12

Monday   **1.** 1   **2.** B   **3.** 24; Arrays should show 8 groups of 3 circles each.   **4.** 30; Sample answer: I have 6 groups of 5 glue sticks.

Tuesday   **1. A.** odd **B.** even   **2. A.** 200 + 40 + 1 **B.** 300 + 80 + 6   **3.** $1.40   **4.** B

Wednesday   **1.** circle   **2.** 5   **3.** sphere   **4.** C   **5.** A

Thursday   **1.** C   **2.** Lines should measure 1 cm.   **3.** 8 units, 3 square units   **4.** C

Friday   **1.** chocolate   **2.** vanilla   **3.** 35   **4.** 65

Brain Stretch   130 stamps

Week 5, pages 13–15

Monday   **1.** 8 + 8 + 8 + 8 = 32, 4 x 8 = 32   **2.** B   **3.** 15   **4.** Boxes should show 5 items in each box.   **5.** 29

Tuesday   **1. A.** 900 + 70 + 4 **B.** 400 + 10 + 3   **2.** 382   **3.** 8 equal parts   **4.** <

Wednesday   **1.** trapezoid   **2.** 4   **3.** square-based pyramid   **4.** B

Thursday   **1.** mm   **2.** Lines should measure 2 cm.   **3.** 14 units, 10 square units   **4.** 5:30, 5:45

Friday   **1.** dog   **2.** bird   **3.** 15   **4.** 1   **5.** 3

Brain Stretch   141 pieces of fruit

Week 6, pages 16–18

Monday   **1.** 2   **2.** A   **3.** 14   **4.** Yes. Model should show 54 ÷ 9.   **5.** 2, 4, 6, 8, 10, 12; even

Tuesday   **1.** ⑥⑦   **2.** Sample answer: 7 + 7 = 14   **3.** 190, 180, 170, 160   **4.** C   **5. A.** 600 + 50 + 1 **B.** 700 + 40 + 2

Wednesday   **1.** quadrilateral or parallelogram   **2.** 4   **3.** rectangular prism   **4.** ⊕   **5.** A

Thursday   1. C   2. 15 minutes   3. 18 units, 10 square units   4. B
Friday   1. Vegetables ||| , Popcorn ||| , Fruit ++++ , Crackers | 2. fruit   3. crackers   4. 12   5. crackers
Brain Stretch   Sample answer: 3 x 8 = 24, 25 − 1 = 24, 12 + 12 = 24

Week 7, pages 19–21

Monday   1. 36   2. A   3. 14   4. $32; Sample answer: 4 groups of 8 fish   5. 72
Tuesday   1. A. 600 B. 2   2. 439   3. 665, 655, 645, 635   4. <   5. Sample answer: 5 + 0 = 5
Wednesday   1. 8   2. 4   3. B   4. B   5. sphere
Thursday   1. B   2. 10 minutes   3. A. 12 B. 4 x 3 = 12   4. −4ºC, 12ºC, 30ºC
Friday   1. 35   2. Oatmeal Raisin   3. 15   4. 10
Brain Stretch   10 triangles

Week 8, pages 22–24

Monday   1. 24; 6; 4; 4   2. C   3. Arrays should show 4 rows of 5 circles each. 20 ÷ 4 = 5
    4. 25, 30, 35; Sample answer: They end in 0 or 5.
Tuesday   1. A. 800 B. 7   2. A   3. A   4. ⊕
Wednesday   1. ◯   2. A   3. cylinder   4. C   5. B
Thursday   1. 1000 metres   2. B   3. Lines should measure 1 1/2 cm.   4. 14 units, 10 square units   5. C
Friday   1. Science Centre ||| , Factory || , Museum ||| , Farm |||| 2. farm   3. farm   4. science centre and museum
    5. 12
Brain Stretch   262 marbles

Week 9, pages 25–27

Monday   1. 14   2. A   3. Arrays should show 3 rows of 6 circles each. 18 ÷ 3 = 6
    4. 30, 36, 42; Multiples of even numbers are even.
Tuesday   1. Sample answer: 6 + 6 + 6 + 6 + 6 = 30   2. >   3. 383, 373, 363, 353   4. ⊞ 4; 1/4
    5. A. 700 + 60 + 6 B. 600 + 40 + 7
Wednesday   1. sphere   2. A polygon is a closed figure with 3 or more straight sides.
    3. Look for a picture of a 4-sided shape.   4. Sample answer: ✝   5. A or C
Thursday   1. B   2. A   3. 14 units, 7 square units   4. A
Friday   1. Nicolette   2. 30   3. Stasia   4. 4
Brain Stretch   24 legs

Week 10, pages 28–30

Monday   1. 5   2. 10   3. 83   4. 6 + 6 + 6 + 6 + 6 = 30, 5 × 6 = 30
Tuesday   1. 467   2. A. 600 + 50 + 1 B. 700 + 60 + 5   3. 135, 140, 145, 150   4. C
    5. five hundred twenty-three   6. 150
Wednesday   1. A quadrilateral is a closed figure with 4 straight sides.   2. Picture should show a quadrilateral and a rhombus.
    Sample answers: A. Both have 4 sides. B. The rhombus has all 4 sides the same length.   3. cube   4. W
    5. C
Thursday   1. B   2. number line: 9:30, 9:40, 9:50; 40 minutes   3. 16 units, 9 square units   4. C
Friday   1. 5   2. 10   3. 5   4. tulips   5. 15
Brain Stretch   36 eggs

Week 11, pages 31–33

Monday   1. 5 × 2 = 10, 2 × 5 = 10   2. Arrays should show 2 rows of 7 circles each. 14 ÷ 2 = 7   3. C
    4. 5; Sample answer: Drawing showing 3 groups of 5 counters.
Tuesday   1. 407   2. A. even B. odd   3. 424, 426, 428, 430   4. 🐋🐋🐋   5. 607 < 670 < 706
    6. All but one part should be coloured.

Wednesday   **1.** pentagon   **2.** A   **3.** cone   **4.** Picture should show a quadrilateral and a parallelogram. Sample answers: A. Both have 4 sides. B. The parallelogram has 2 pairs of parallel sides.   **5.** ⬭⬠⬯▽◯

Thursday   **1.** A   **2.** Lines should measure 2 cm.   **3.** 16 units, 12 square units   **4.** B

Friday   **1.** Mr. Patel   **2.** Ms. Apor and Ms. Rocco   **3.** Ms. Rocco   **4.** Mr. Patel   **5.** Ms. Apor and Ms. Rocco

Brain Stretch   Sample answer: Arrays should show 2 rows of 15 circles/tulips each. 30 ÷ 2 = 15; Arrays should show 5 rows of 6 circles/tulips each. 30 ÷ 5 = 6

Week 12, pages 34–36

Monday   **1.** 11   **2.** B   **3.** Arrays should show 5 rows of 5 circles each. 25 ÷ 5 = 5
4. Yes. Sample answer: 10 × 1 = 10; 10 × 2 = 20; 10 × 3 = 30. All the products end in 0.   **5.** 21

Tuesday   **1.** Estimate: 800; Sum: 859   **2. A.** even **B.** odd   **3.** 5   **4.** 234   **5.** 901 > 899 > 818
6. One part of the shape should be coloured.

Wednesday   **1.** Answers could include: square, rectangle, quadrilateral, rhombus   **2.** 6   **3.** 2   **4.** B
5. ◯⬡⬯△◯

Thursday   **1.** a scale   **2.** A   **3.** 14 units, 8 square units   **4.** C

Friday   **1.** Shading should extend to 5 for cereal, 15 for eggs, 20 for pancakes, and 15 for grilled cheese
2. pancakes   **3.** 25   **4.** eggs and grilled cheese   **5.** 10

Brain Stretch   **1.** 1006   **2.** 536   **3.** 921   **4.** 346

Week 13, pages 37–39

Monday   **1.** 18; The pattern increases by 3 between each term.   **2.** B   **3.** 8   **4.** growing   **5.** 37

Tuesday   **1.** 60   **2.** 3; 1/3   **3. A.** $3.60 **B.** $20.05   **4.** <   **5.** C

Wednesday   **1.** Accept any shape with 4 sides that is not a rectangle.   **2.** 3   **3.** 0   **4.** B   **5.** B

Thursday   **1.** 12:30   **2.** 16 units, 11 square units   **3.** A   **4.** –3ºC, 12ºC, 33ºC

Friday   **1.** Friday   **2.** Monday   **3.** The number of fish caught increases by 2 each day.   **4.** 12   **5.** 8

Brain Stretch   143 tulip bulbs

Week 14, pages 40–42

Monday   **1.** 141   **2.** B   **3.** 37, 42, 47   **4.** repeating   **5.** 62

Tuesday   **1.** fifty   **2.** 911, 921, 931, 941   **3.** 1/3 pizza; Thirds are larger than fifths.   **4.** 🐟🐟🐟   **5.** 267

Wednesday   **1.** Accept any shape with 4 sides.   **2.** Accept any shape that does not have 4 sides.   **3.** 12
4. A or B   **5.** A

Thursday   **1.** 4:30   **2.** 12 units, 5 square units   **3.** B   **4.** A

Friday   Favourite Season Graph title: Favourite Season Survey; Y axis title: Number of Votes; X axis title: Season; Shading should extend to 10 for spring, 15 for summer, 25 for autumn, and 15 for winter.
1. autumn, summer and winter, spring   **2.** 5   **3.** 40

Brain Stretch   590 stamps

Week 15, pages 43–45

Monday   **1.** 57   **2.** B   **3.** 27; Arrays should show 3 rows of 9 circles each.   **4.** 350
5. Any number multiplied by 0 equals 0.

Tuesday   **1.** 522   **2.** Sample answer: 7 + 7 + 7 + 7 + 7 + 7 = 42   **3. A.** 90 **B.** 30
4. Sample answer: ▭▭▭   **5.** 944

Wednesday   **1.** Accept any four-sided figure with two parallel sides.   **2.** 0   **3.** 1   **4.** A   **5.** A

Thursday   **1.** 6:35   **2.** 16 square units, 12 square units   **3.** 2, 8, 2, 6; 6, 14 square units   **4.** 2 litres

Friday   Numbers in the favourite farm animal chart should be 11 for chickens, 4 for cows, 13 for pigs, 17 for horses, and 4 for sheep   **1.** 49   **2.** horses   **3.** 13   **4.** 2   **5.** 24

Brain Stretch   50 books

Week 16, pages 46–48

Monday   **1.** 1; 2; 3; 4; 5; 6; Multiplying a number by 1 results in the number itself.   **2.** A   **3.** 46
4. Arrays should show 5 rows of 6 circles each. 30 ÷ 5 = 6

Tuesday   **1. A.** 700 **B.** 400   **2.** $4.25, $2.10   **3. B.** 87   **4.** 732

Wednesday   **1.** Accept any stackable 3D figure such as a cube or rectangular prism.   **2.** 8   **3.** 5   **4.** C
5.

Thursday   **1.** millimetres or centimetres   **2.** 35 square cm   **3.** 14 units, 7 square units   **4. A.** litre **B.** millilitre

Friday   **1.** 12   **2.** 24   **3.** 15   **4.** 9   **5.** basketball, hockey, soccer

Brain Stretch   Accept any combination of quarters and dimes that adds up to $1.70, such as 6 quarters and 2 dimes.

Week 17, pages 49–51

Monday   **1.** A   **2.** B   **3.** shrinking   **4.** Arrays should show 4 rows of 7 circles each. 28 ÷ 4 = 7   **5.** 28

Tuesday   **1.** 943   **2.** 50, 80, 20   **3.** 1/8   **4.** (5¢)(5¢)(5¢)   **5.**

Wednesday   **1.** The same size and shape.   **2.** Picture should show a rectangle and a square. **A.** Both have all right
angles. **B.** A square has 4 sides the same length.   **3.** 8   **4.** A   **5.** B

Thursday   **1.** B   **2.** A   **3.** 14 units, 10 square units   **4.** 24 cups

Friday   **1.** 5   **2.** Thursday   **3.** 28th   **4.** 8th   **5.** Wednesday

Brain Stretch   6 groups of trophies

Week 18, pages 52–54

Monday   **1.** 663   **2.** A   **3.** 9 × 4 = 36, 36 ÷ 9 = 4, 36 ÷ 4 = 9   **4.** 100, 125, 150   **5.** 5

Tuesday   **1. A.** 40 **B.** 60 **C.** 90   **2.** A   **3.** 3500, 3600, 3700   **4.** 863   **5.** Estimate: 550; Difference: 562

Wednesday   **1.** triangle.   **2.**   **3.** 12   **4.** 0   **5.**

Thursday   **1.** B   **2.** B   **3.** 18 units, 12 square units   **4.** 22ºC, 6ºC, –8ºC

Friday   **1.** 4   **2.** Thursday   **3.** August 25th   **4.** 20th   **5.** Saturday

Brain Stretch   14 marbles

Week 19, pages 55–57

Monday   **1.** 800   **2.** B   **3.** 5   **4.** 7   **5.** 42

Tuesday   **1. A.** 500 + 30 + 1 **B.** 200 + 10 + 4   **2.** =   **3.** 858, 859, 860, 861   **4. A.** $4.14 **B.** $0.82   **5.**

Wednesday   **1.** circle   **2.** B   **3.** 6   **4.** 0   **5.** C

Thursday   **1.** 16 units, 9 square units   **2.** 6:30, 6:00   **3.** 30ºC, 15ºC, –5ºC   **4.** B

Friday   **1.** skipping   **2.** hopscotch, tag   **3.** baseball   **4.** baseball, basketball, hopscotch and tag, skipping

Brain Stretch   4 boxes

Week 20, pages 58–60

Monday   **1.** 59   **2.** B   **3.** 7   **4.** repeating   **5.** 40

Tuesday   **1.** (25¢)(25¢)(5¢)   **2. A.** 170 **B.** 720   **3.** 125, 150, 175, 200   **4.** Estimate: 150; Difference: 193
5. 638 > 312 > 244 > 12

Wednesday   **1.** square   **2.** A or C   **3.** 2   **4.** 0   **5.**

Thursday   **1.** C   **2.** 5:25   **3.** 16 units, 9 square units
4. 3 square units and 6 square units and 9 square units

Friday   **1.** 30   **2.** pineapple   **3.** pineapple, apple, grape, orange   **4.** 24

Brain Stretch   2/3 of the hair ribbons are blue

Week 21, pages 61–63

Monday   **1.** 90   **2.** B   **3.** 3 × 7 + d = 30; d = 9 km   **4.** 3 × 9 = 27, 9 × 3 = 27

Tuesday   **1.** 720   **2.** 674, 673, 672, 671   **3.** eight hundred eighty-eight   **4. A.** 20 **B.** 70
5. $1.45   **6.** >

Wednesday   1. octagon   2. Sample answer: 3. 0   4.
Thursday   1. 3:20   2. 16 units, 7 square units   3. C   4. B
Friday   1. 12   2. 16   3. mall   4. library   5. library, zoo, circus, park, mall
Brain Stretch   21 L

Week 22, pages 64–66

Monday   1. 73   2. B   3. $h = 5$ 4. 70
Tuesday   1. 5   2. 150   3. 216   4. 241   5. 1/5
Wednesday   1. sphere   2. B   3. 8   4. 1   5. B
Thursday   1. 1:10   2. 29ºC, 8ºC, −10ºC   3. 16 cm   4. 9 square units
Friday   Shading on the Favourite Season Graph should extend to 35 for spring, 50 for summer, 40 for autumn, and 20 for winter; X axis title: Number of Votes; Category: Summer; X axis scale: 20, 25, 30, 35, 40, 45, 50
   1. 70   2. Summer   3. Summer, Autumn, Spring, Winter   4. 5
Brain Stretch   A rectangle and a square both have 4 sides, 4 vertices, 4 right angles, and 2 pairs of parallel sides.

Week 23, pages 67–69

Monday   1. 778   2. C   3. 61   4. G
Tuesday   1. A. $7.50 B. $0.90   2. A. 40 B. 60   3. 56   4. 80   5. 2/7
Wednesday   1. Sample answer: 2. rectangle   3.   4. 8   5.
Thursday   1. C   2. Lines should measure 4 cm.   3. 16 units, 13 square units   4. 2:00
Friday   1. 26   2. 12   3. 32   4. 82
Brain Stretch   A parallelogram and triangle have different numbers of sides and vertices, and a parallelogram has 2 pairs of parallel sides but a triangle has no parallel sides.

Week 24, pages 70–72

Monday   1. 40   2. A   3. 10   4. 12, 6, 20   5. A. I rounded 123 to 100, 43 to 50, and 91 to 100. That makes 250 stamps. B. 257
Tuesday   1. 8   2. 811   3. A. odd B. even   4.
   5.
Wednesday   1. rectangular prism   2. B   3. 8   4. Sample answer: 5.
Thursday   1. B   2. A   3. 16 units, 11 square units   4. 3:50
Friday   1. 4   2. Monday   3. November 17th   4. November 18th   5. Friday
Brain Stretch   Accept any 6 number sentences that each have a difference of 5.

Week 25, pages 73–75

Monday   1. 485   2. repeating pattern   3. 7, 6   4. 6, 8, 3
Tuesday   1. Estimate: 750; Sum: 740   2. 943   3. 44   4. 10   5. >   6. Sample answer: 9 + 9 + 9 = 27
Wednesday   1. Sample answer: 2.   3. 1   4. C   5. C
Thursday   1. B   2. A   3. 20 units, 10 square units   4. 11:00
Friday   1. Monday   2. 5   3. Sunday   4. 14th   5. 5th
Brain Stretch   1. 50   2. 36   3. 30   4. 9   5. 9   6. 8   7. 24   8. 7   9. 10   10. 7   11. 1   12. 56

Week 26, pages 76–78

Monday   1. 63   2. B   3. <   4. 80, 31, 19   5. Double the previous number.
Tuesday   1. 240   2. 2/7   4. 3/4   5. A. 20 B. 50
Wednesday   1. Accept any lines that cross each other.   2. A   3. 1   4.   5.
Thursday   1. 6:45   2. A   3. 16 units   4. 8 square units   5. C
Friday   1. 4   2. 12   3. clothes   4. 4
Brain Stretch   1. 35   2. 14   3. 81   4. 5   5. 72   6. 10   7. 36   8. 10   9. 10   10. 7   11. 5   12. 36

Week 27, pages 79–81

Monday   **1.** 88   **2.** A   **3.** $h = 8$ **4.** 211, 467, 85   **5.** 82, 80, 78

Tuesday   **1.** Estimate: 650; Sum: 633   **2. A.** 821 **B.** 437   **3.** 775, 800, 825, 850   **4.** 234   **5.** >

Wednesday   **1.** Sample answers: can, tube   **2.** Sample answer: ◺   **3.** circle   **4.** Sample answer: ⬠   **5.** C

Thursday   **1.** 36   **2.** 7:00   **3.** 9 square units   **4.** 22 units   **5.** 1000 m

Friday   Graph title: Favourite Book Genre; Y axis title: Number of Votes; Y axis scale: 2, 4, 6, 8, 10, 12, 14, 16, 18; X axis title: Book Genres; X axis labels: Mystery, Non-fiction, Fiction, Biography, Adventure; Shading should extend to 12 for mystery, 8 for non-fiction, 8 for fiction, 15 for biography, and 4 for adventure.
1. biography   **2.** biography, mystery, non-fiction and fiction, adventure   **3.** 2   **4.** About 50   **5.** Sample answer: A biography is the most popular genre. More students might read the book.

Brain Stretch   45¢

Week 28, pages 82–84

Monday   **1.** 250   **2.** C   **3.** 10, 10, 80   **4.** B   **5.** 64

Tuesday   **1.** 377   **2. A.** 200 **B.** 600 **C.** 500   **3.** 5/8   **4.** A   **5.** (🐢 🐢 🐢 🐢 🐢)

Wednesday   **1.** Sample answers: a pylon or ice cream cone   **2.** B   **3.** 6   **4.** A or B   **5.** ▱ ⓞ ◹ ⏢ ▭

Thursday   **1.** 16 m²   **2.** 6:05   **3.** 45 units   **4.** 12 units

Friday   **1.** 18   **2.** 16   **3.** trading cards   **4.** 30   **5.** 20

Brain Stretch   **1.** 40   **2.** 21   **3.** 10   **4.** 5   **5.** 90   **6.** 10   **7.** 42   **8.** 3   **9.** 3   **10.** 9   **11.** 7   **12.** 8

Week 29, pages 85–87

Monday   **1.** 300   **2.** B   **3.** 7, 7, 35   **4.** 877, 189, 203   **5.** subtract 3

Tuesday   **1.** Estimate: 200; Difference: 175   **2.** 633   **3.** 4   **4.** A   **5.** 3/6   **6.** 280

Wednesday   **1.** Sample answers: a die or box   **2.** Picture should show a square and a rectangle. **A.** Both have 4 right angles and 2 pairs of parallel sides. **B.** A square has 4 equal sides.   **3.** 1   **4.** B
5. (◹ ⬡ ⏢ △ ⓞ)

Thursday   **1.** 49 days   **2.** 8 units   **3.** 11 square units   **4.** 12 units   **5.** 180 minutes

Friday   Graph title: Favourite School Subject; Y axis title: Number of Votes; Y axis scale: 5, 10, 15, 20, 25, 30, 35, 40; X axis title: Subject; X axis labels: Reading, Art, Math, Science, Music; Shading should extend to 35 for reading, 25 for art, 15 for math, 10 for science, and 20 for music. Sample sentences: The most popular subject is reading. More students like art than music.

Brain Stretch   15 pages

Week 30, pages 88–90

Monday   **1.** 58   **2.** B   **3.** 5, 5   **4.** C   **5.** repeating

Tuesday   **1.** Estimate: 700; Difference: 703   **2. A.** Dana: 170 + 180 = 350 Nathan: 200 + 200 = 400; **B.** 347; Dana
3. A. $9.00 **B.** $0.75   **4.** (💲💲💲💲💲💲💲💲💲)

Wednesday   **1.** Accept any 2 parallel lines.   **2.** Picture should show a square and a rhombus. **A.** Both have 4 equal sides. **B.** A square has 4 right angles.   **3.** B   **4.** ▱ ⬡ ⏢ △ ⓞ

Thursday   **1.** Lines should measure 1.5 cm.   **2.** 4:30   **3.** Sample answer: **A.** 12 square units **B.** divide into 2 rectangles: 9 + 3 = 12 square units   **4.** 20 m

Friday   Graph title: Favourite Pizza Toppings; Y axis title: Number of Votes; Y axis scale: 5, 10, 15, 20, 25, 30, 35, 40; X axis title: Topping; X axis labels: Cheese, Pepperoni, Vegetables, Other; Shading should extend to 25 for cheese, 15 for pepperoni, 35 for vegetables, and 20 for other. Sample sentences: The most popular topping is vegetables. More students like cheese than pepperoni.

Brain Stretch $1.70

www.ingramcontent.com/pod-product-compliance
Lightning Source LLC
Chambersburg PA
CBHW081343090426

42737CB00017B/3268